T0393026

Cambridge Elements

Elements in Experimental Political Science
edited by
James N. Druckman
University of Rochester

INSIDE THE RADICALIZED MIND

The Neuropolitics of Terrorism and Violent Extremism

Tiffiany Howard
University of Nevada, Las Vegas

CAMBRIDGE
UNIVERSITY PRESS

Shaftesbury Road, Cambridge CB2 8EA, United Kingdom

One Liberty Plaza, 20th Floor, New York, NY 10006, USA

477 Williamstown Road, Port Melbourne, VIC 3207, Australia

314–321, 3rd Floor, Plot 3, Splendor Forum, Jasola District Centre,
New Delhi – 110025, India

103 Penang Road, #05–06/07, Visioncrest Commercial, Singapore 238467

Cambridge University Press is part of Cambridge University Press & Assessment,
a department of the University of Cambridge.

We share the University's mission to contribute to society through the pursuit of
education, learning and research at the highest international levels of excellence.

www.cambridge.org
Information on this title: www.cambridge.org/9781009586214

DOI: 10.1017/9781009586207

When citing this work, please include a reference to the DOI 10.1017/9781009586207

First published 2025

A catalogue record for this publication is available from the British Library

ISBN 978-1-009-58621-4 Hardback
ISBN 978-1-009-58617-7 Paperback
ISSN 2633-3368 (online)
ISSN 2633-335X (print)

Additional resources for this publication at www.cambridge.org/howard

Inside the Radicalized Mind

The Neuropolitics of Terrorism and Violent Extremism

Elements in Experimental Political Science

DOI: 10.1017/9781009586207
First published online: March 2025

Tiffiany Howard
University of Nevada, Las Vegas
Author for correspondence: Tiffiany Howard, tiffiany.howard@unlv.edu

Abstract: This Element aims to better understand the role of the internet in the radicalization process, focusing on how online factors contribute to self-radicalization. Specifically, it examines the neurocognitive process of online radicalization by analyzing the impact of terrorist and extremist propaganda videos on individuals' cognitive empathy using electroencephalography (EEG). Ultimately, this research aims to provide a more comprehensive understanding of online radicalization and the psychological effects of exposure to extremist content on the internet.

Keywords: neuropolitics, political neuroscience, online internet radicalization, extremism, terrorism, political violence, emotions, cognitive empathy, social psychology, experimental political science methods

ISBNs: 9781009586214 (HB), 9781009586177 (PB), 9781009586207 (OC)
ISSNs: 2633-3368 (online), 2633-335X (print)

Contents

1 Introduction: The Radicalized Mind

On June 12, 2016, Omar Mateen, a 29-year-old U.S.-born man, entered Pulse Nightclub in Orlando, Florida, and opened fire, killing 49 people and injuring 53 others. Before the attack, he called 911 to pledge allegiance to ISIS. At that time, it was the deadliest mass shooting in U.S. history (Elmasry and el-Nawawy, 2020). Nearly six years later, on May 14, 2022, 18-year-old white supremacist Payton S. Gendron drove over 200 miles to a Buffalo, New York, grocery store in a predominantly Black neighborhood and killed 10 African Americans (Benton and Benton, 2023).

Despite their differing ideologies, both men were radicalized online after consuming hours of extremist content on platforms like YouTube, Facebook, and X (formerly Twitter). Mateen was self-radicalized through jihadist propaganda, including beheading videos (Swisher et al., 2016; Parker, 2020). Gendron's writings link his radicalization to over 100 YouTube videos, which also helped him plan his attack (Benton and Benton, 2023).

The internet has altered traditional radicalization processes and pathways, and we are only beginning to fully understand the extent of its impact. Prior to 9/11, an individual was introduced to an extremist ideology by an associate, friend, or relative that helped usher them into the world of the terrorist organization. Of course there are always exceptions, the most well-known being that of the Oklahoma City bomber, Timothy McVeigh, who many argue was predominantly self-radicalized (Rajakuma, 2013), although, there are some scholars who disagree, and assert that while he operated as a lone actor, his pathway to radicalization was a combination of traditional and self-radicalization processes (Sprinzak, 2001; Springer, 2009; Spaaij, 2012; Gill 2015). However, if one believes the prevailing assumption, that McVeigh was indeed self-radicalized, then he represents an outlier given what we know of terrorist recruitment and radicalization networks, and how they operated before 9/11.

During the post-9/11 era, we began to observe a shift in the radicalization process given the growing influence of the internet. After 9/11, an alternative radicalization pathway started to emerge. On the one hand, the traditional pathway, where an individual is initially exposed to extremism through a known, in-person contact, remained salient. However, a second pathway also began to take root. In this case, during the first stage of the process, an individual would establish contact and connections with other extremist sympathizers on the internet, particularly on message boards and in online forums, which was the result of the rise in popularity of social networking sites (MySpace, Friendster, Facebook, etc.). This first stage is what we as terrorism scholars would begin to identify as self-radicalization. However, at that time in history, self-radicalization would not typically lead to the culmination of any violent act. Therefore, the radicalization process would not be considered complete until that individual made direct contact with a member of an extremist or terrorist organization, which would often involve traveling abroad for training, and full indoctrination.

It wasn't until the late 2000s and early 2010s, when social networking was augmented by social media (YouTube, X/Twitter, Instagram, etc.), that we began to witness a fundamental transformation in the radicalization process. While the traditional radicalization process remains intact, there has been a notable increase in the frequency and lethality of extremist attacks committed by individuals who have never made or had any direct contact (in-person or otherwise) with an extremist group or any of its members. Instead, they have been self-radicalized by exposure to extremist propaganda on the internet (Parker, 2020).

1.1 Main Purpose and Study Aim

This Element aims to better understand the role of the internet in the radicalization process, focusing on how online factors contribute to self-radicalization. Specifically, I examine the neurocognitive process of online radicalization by analyzing the impact of extremist propaganda videos on individuals' cognitive empathy using electroencephalography (EEG). This study explores the relationship between empathy and online propaganda, highlighting how high levels of empathy for in-group members can lead to decreased empathy for out-group members, potentially driving radicalization and violent extremism (Campbell and Babrow, 2004; Feddes et al., 2015; Bruneau, 2016; Howard et al., 2019, 2022; Zmigrod et al., 2019; Zmigrod, 2020; Schumann et al., 2022; Obaidi et al., 2023). Ultimately, this research aims to provide a more comprehensive understanding of online radicalization and the psychological effects of exposure to extremist content on the internet.

1.2 Structure of the Element

Inside the Radicalized Mind is structured into six sections, beginning with this Introduction. Section 2 reviews the literature on radicalization, extremism, and terrorism, defining radicalization and outlining the process of indoctrination. This section distinguishes extremist violence from other forms of violence, highlighting the two primary outcomes of radicalization today: radical Islamic terrorism and right-wing/alt-right extremism. By the end of this section, a clear understanding of radicalization and its key outcomes is established.

Section 3 builds upon the literature by presenting the theoretical foundation of the study, using Kruglanski et al.'s (2019, 2022b) 3 N Model (i.e. The Need,

The Narrative and The Network), which posits that radicalization results from the interplay of personal needs, extremist narratives, and social networks.

Section 4 covers data acquisition, experimental procedures, and methodology. It details the questionnaires used to assess participants' empathy, the selection of stimulus videos, recruitment processes, study demographics, and the use of EEG to capture neural responses to stimuli.

Section 5 focuses on data analysis and presenting findings from the questionnaires and EEG experiments. It concludes with a discussion of the findings.

In Section 6, I explore the implications of these findings within the broader context of neuropolitics, political extremism, and terrorism. The section ends with a discussion of the study's weaknesses and limitations, its contributions to neuropolitics research, and suggestions for future cross-disciplinary studies on radicalization, terrorism, and extremism.

2 Review of the Literature

What drives an individual to adopt extremist beliefs and engage in violent extremism? These are key questions in social sciences, with existing studies shedding light on the processes of radicalization and violent action (Cavanaugh, 2012). Despite extensive research across social science, security, and policy fields, there is no consensus on the radicalization process (O'Loughlin et al., 2011; Borum, 2011; Kundnani, 2012; Heath-Kelly, 2013). However, it is widely acknowledged that radicalization is a dynamic process influenced by a mix of social, economic, political, ideological, historical, and psychological factors (Office of the National Security Advisor, 2015).

This section reviews the literature to define radicalization, outline its process, identify key causes, and examine its outcomes.

2.1 The Concept and Process of Radicalization

Radicalization is widely recognized as a dynamic, nonlinear process in which an individual adopts beliefs that justify the use of violence for societal change (McCauley and Moskalenko, 2008, 2010; Borum, 2011; Maskaliūnaitė, 2015; Della Porta and LaFree, 2012; Christmann, 2012). While scholars agree on its processual nature, they differ on its specifics. Christmann's review of 310 studies from 1987 to 2010 supports this consensus but highlights significant variation in how the process is conceptualized (2012).

The radicalization process is complex, involving both internal and external influences that vary by individual. Some scholars describe this process in several stages, while others outline fewer steps. For example, McCauley and Moskalenko (2008) define twelve dimensions of radicalization (Table 1),

Table 1 McCauley and Moskalenko's twelve mechanisms of radicalization

Level of Radicalization	Mechanism
Individual	
	1. Personal victimization
	2. Political grievance
	3. Joining a radical group – slippery slope
	4. Joining a radical group – power of love
	5. Extremity shift in like-minded groups
Group	
	6. Extreme cohesion under isolation and threat
	7. Competition for the same base of support
	8. Competition with state power
	9. Within group competition – fissioning
Mass	
	10. Jujitsu politics
	11. Hate
	12. Martyrdom

Table 2 Taarnby's eight-stage recruitment process

1. Individual alienation and marginalization
2. A spiritual quest
3. A process of radicalization
4. Meeting and associating with like-minded people
5. Gradual seclusion and cell formation
6. Acceptance of violence as legitimate political means
7. Connection with a gatekeeper in the know
8. Going operational

Taarnby (2005) sees it as an eight-stage recruitment process (Table 2), and Moghaddam (2005) presents a staircase model that portrays radicalization as a progression from perception of inequality to readiness for violence.

Moghaddam's staircase model illustrates radicalization as a journey from a broad societal base to the narrow pinnacle of terrorism. At the ground level, individuals focus on perceived inequality. As they ascend, they move from seeking solutions (first floor) to displacing aggression (second floor), joining extremist groups (third floor), undergoing indoctrination (fourth floor), and, finally, being ready to commit violence (fifth floor).

A more recent, condensed model of Moghaddam's approach integrates de-radicalization and three levels of engagement (micro, meso, macro), summarizing radicalization into three phases: sensitivity to extreme ideology, recruitment, and readiness for violence (Figure 1) (Doosje et al., 2016).

The works of McCauley and Moskalenko (2008), Taarnby (2005), Moghaddam (2005), and Doosje et al. (2016) contribute to our understanding of radicalization by identifying specific mechanisms that propel individuals along the radicalization spectrum.

Most research organizes radicalization into four key stages: preradicalization, identification, intensification/indoctrination, and radicalization (beliefs and/or action). Though terms and stages may vary, the underlying process remains consistent across various models (see Online Appendix Tables 12 and 13 and Figure 22; Sageman, 2004; Gill, 2017; Silber and Bhatt, 2007; Christmann, 2012).

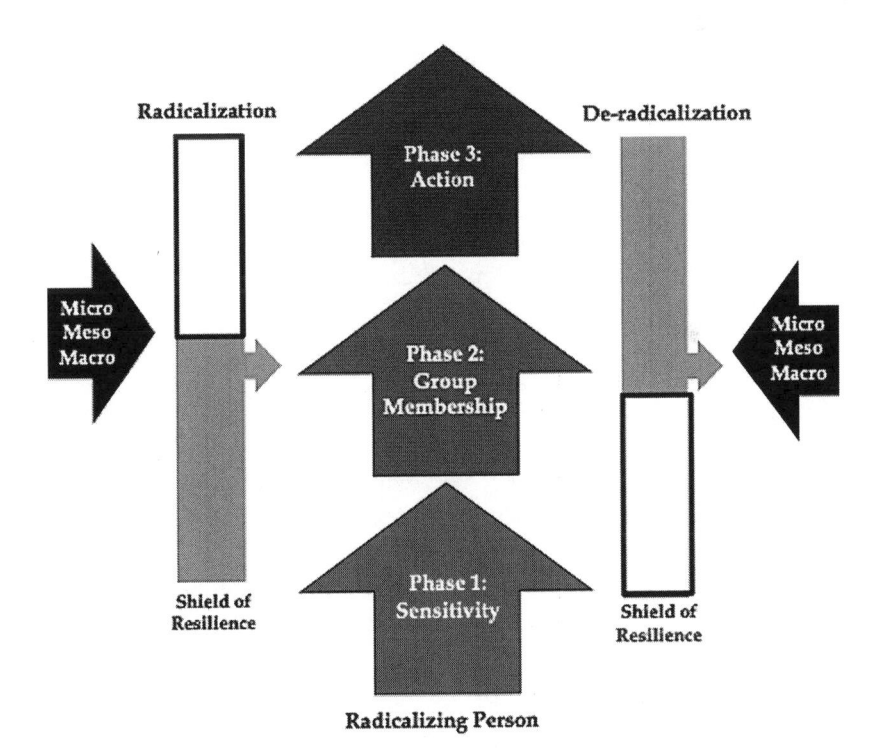

Figure 1 Moghaddam's staircase model–inspired three-phase process of radicalization

Source: Doosji, Bertijan, Fathali M. Moghaddam, Arie W. Kruglanski, Arjan de Wolf, Liesbeth Mann, and Allard R. Feddes. (2016). "Terrorism, Radicalization and De-radicalization." *Current Opinion in Psychology,* 11 (June): 79–84. www.sciencedirect .com/science/article/pii/S2352250X16300811.

2.1.1 The Four Stages of Radicalization

1. **Pre-Radicalization:** At this stage, a person may be aware of extremist groups and have a basic understanding of certain ideologies but has not yet been exposed to an extremist group or its beliefs. Some believe that external (social, political, economic) and internal (psychological, familial, personal) factors may make certain individuals more vulnerable during this stage (Howard et al., 2019). This stage corresponds to Moghaddam's "ground floor," where most people remain (2005).

2. **Identification:** In this stage, a person begins to identify with a specific belief system or group. The transition from Pre-Radicalization to Identification is often triggered by personal or external factors. Personal triggers might include a breakup, job loss, the death of a loved one, or victimization. External triggers could be foreign occupation, recession, terrorist attacks, social upheaval, or group dissidence.

3. **Intensification and Indoctrination:** Here, a person's commitment to extremist beliefs deepens, leading to either internal affirmation or external commitment, such as formally joining an extremist group.

4. **Radicalization:** In the final stage, a person fully embraces an extremist belief system, endorses or engages in violence for the cause, and is considered fully radicalized. This individual is now psychologically prepared and capable of committing violence, regardless of whether they act on it.

Given the scope of this study, this experiment is designed to capture the identification stage of the radicalization process. While every phase in the four-stage process is important, there are limitations to this type of experimental research and its ability to assess an individual at other stages along the radicalization process. I consider the identification stage of the process to be the most pivotal, because it is during this period that a person sets out on the pathway that ultimately leads to radicalization. It is also the point when diversion has the greatest probability of success (McDowell-Smith et al., 2017). Therefore, gaining insight into the neural processes that are at play when an individual begins to identify with and absorb extremist messaging into their psyche represents an important contribution to the deradicalization scholarship as well.

2.2 Radicalization: The Causes

In the preceding subsection (Section 2.1), I discuss the concept of radicalization, highlighting internal and external factors that align with existing literature. Here, I consolidate key theories identifying social, economic, and political root causes, along with individual risk factors, focusing on social-psychological and social-neuroscientific perspectives.

2.2.1 Social Factors

Sociologists have theorized that radicalization and political violence stem from collective action fueled by grievances, political opportunity, discontent, and organizational capacity (Tilly, 2003; Boyns and Ballard, 2004, p. 11; Oberschall, 2004). Six key theoretical propositions support this view. The first suggests that violent political behavior arises from societal structures that enforce hegemonic dominance, creating divisions between the powerful and powerless. This dynamic leads to social stress and the emergence of radical political beliefs and actions (Clegg, 1989; Boyns and Ballard, 2004).

The second proposition suggests that extremism and terrorism stem from power–prestige dynamics, serving as a means for groups with power deficits to boost their prestige (Weber, 1946; Collins, 1986). The third proposition asserts that organizations are resource-dependent; the need for material resources sparks the formation of terrorist and extremist groups, and greater resource availability enables them to operate and carry out attacks (McCarthy and Zald, 1977; Jenkins, 1983).

The fourth proposition asserts that terrorism and extremism are byproducts of intragroup conflict. The fifth proposition views political violence as an inevitable social ritual that reinforces cultural beliefs and practices of nonnormative behavior, drawing heavily on Durkheim's work on social rituals and group solidarity (Durkheim, 1984[1893], 1995[1912]). Simmel (1955[1908]) and Coser (1956) refine Durkheim's theory, laying the groundwork for the sixth theory, which argues that political violence fosters solidarity in both dominant and opposing groups, a fundamental aspect of all societies (Collins, 2004).

2.2.2 Economic Factors

Economists and International Political Economy (IPE) scholars argue that economic factors are at the root of extremist beliefs and violent political behavior. Consequently, these scholars identify poverty and economic conditions, as well as the lack of education as key inciters of violent extremism (Fearon and Laitin, 2003; Azam and Delacroix, 2006; Lai, 2007; Azam and Thelen, 2008; Hess and Blomberg, 2008). Most notably, Newman finds that "poverty breeds resentment" which can lead to desperation that eventually results in political violence (2006, p. 751). On the other hand, while economic choice models identify a link between economic conditions and violent political behavior, this vein of scholarship finds that poverty is not the driver, and instead points to lost economic opportunities, especially among the highly educated and high skilled individuals, which creates incentives for radical behavior (Krueger and Malečková, 2003; Krueger, 2007; Enders and Sandler, 2011, 2012). Similarly, Blair et al. find that impoverished classes may even be more hostile to utilizing violent extremism to achieve one's aims in comparison to higher class individuals with grievances (2013).

On the opposite end of the spectrum, there are several studies of economic factors which find very weak evidence, or none at all, in support of poverty, a lack of education, and other measures of poor economic conditions as the root causes of radicalization and violent political behavior (Kurrild-Klitgaard et al., 2006; Berrebi, 2007; Piazza, 2007; Freytag et al., 2009).

2.2.3 Political Factors

Early political science research on terrorism has focused heavily on grievances as a key cause. Gurr's theory of relative deprivation highlights how sociopolitical discontent drives political violence, rebellion, and terrorism that are rooted in frustration when societal expectations are unmet (1970). While this theory remains relevant, more contemporary studies suggest that aggression from feelings of humiliation, distress, and hopelessness may be even stronger motivators (Speckhard, 2008; Vertigans, 2013; McCauley and Moskalenko, 2017b).

Crenshaw (1998, 2012) adds nuance by arguing that violent political behavior often stems not just from broad sociopolitical or material deprivation, but from the disaffection of a small elite acting on behalf of a larger group. She notes that in modern states with unresponsive bureaucracies, terrorism becomes an appealing tactic to attract support, intimidate opponents, or achieve political goals (2012, p. 11).

Finally, scholars who are focused on political antecedents have argued that foreign occupation is the catalyst for radicalization and terrorism (Pape, 2005), or point to weak, failing, and failed states, with their inherent physical and material insecurity, arguing that they provide fertile ground for extremism (Howard, 2008; Piazza, 2008).

2.2.4 Summary of the Traditional Social Science Causes of Radicalization

This discussion is not an exhaustive review of the radicalization, extremism, and terrorism literature, but rather highlights the key social science theories and their overemphasis on the structural drivers of radicalization and violent political behavior. Despite widespread poverty, oppression, deprivation, and powerlessness, millions of people do not resort to violent extremism or terrorism (Krueger and Malečková, 2003; Newman, 2006). This is because adopting extremist beliefs is fundamentally a psychological process.

Undoubtedly, the psychological process of adopting an extremist belief system is shaped by one's social, economic, and political condition, which is why increasingly the radicalization, extremism, and terrorism literatures have been informed by interdisciplinary approaches that provide a more comprehensive treatment of these phenomena. Two of the more prominent perspectives to emerge in response to a need for more cross-disciplinary explanations for radicalization and political violence have been social psychology and social neuroscience, and their theoretical frameworks are examined in the following sections.

2.2.5 Social-Psychological Factors

Social-psychological perspectives focus on how an individual's mindset is shaped by their relationships and environment, and how this mindset influences their self-view within their social circle and society. Moghaddam's (2005) staircase model, which likens radicalization to ascending a narrowing staircase, is a key model in social psychology, emphasizing the importance of the person-situation interaction in understanding radicalization and extremist behavior (Lemieux, 2006).

Building on this, social identity theory (SIT) highlights the need to examine radicalization through the convergence of individual and group identities. SIT posits that individuals possess multiple identities shaped by the groups they belong to, known as in-groups. This dual identity – personal and social – is crucial in the radicalization process, as extremist groups exploit in-group identities with propaganda that fosters negative views of out-group members (Roessing and Siebert, 2006; Baines et al., 2010; Rieger et al., 2020).

According to SIT, effective communication between extremist organizations and potential supporters relies on clear group identification, recognized by both in-group and out-group members (Tajfel and Turner, 1986). This is because social identity is shaped through social comparison, which involves two key processes: intragroup comparison (evaluating members within the same group) and inter-group comparison (comparing one's group to others) (Rieger et al., 2020, p. 283). These comparisons provide feedback on an individual's sense of worth, value, and social status, informing their social identity (Branscombe and Wann, 1994).

While SIT doesn't explicitly discuss "push" and "pull" dynamics, these concepts are inherent in the formation of individual and group identities, which can both attract (pull) and drive (push) individuals toward extremism and terrorism. SIT scholars categorize these motivational factors into two themes: self-esteem and uncertainty-identity factors (Sherif, 1966; Staub, 1989, 2003; Sidanius and Pratto, 1999; Lemieux and Pratto, 2003; Hewstone et al., 2004; Rieger et al., 2020).

The self-esteem premise suggests that individuals assign positive value to their in-group and negative value to out-groups to maintain their self-esteem. Self-esteem is considered a basic human need (see Maslow's Hierarchy of Needs, 1954), so when something or someone challenges an individual's value judgments regarding their in-group and out-group(s), this can negatively affect self-esteem. Also, because group membership can address an individual's needs at every level of Maslow's hierarchy, from safety and security, to self-actualization, a person can be motivated to identify with an extremist group or ideology because it provides an in-group counter-narrative that serves to elevate their self-esteem (1954; Strindberg, 2020). Thus, low self-esteem can act as a push factor, while the esteem-building benefits of group identification represent a pull factor.

The uncertainty-identity premise posits that individuals need to understand their societal role, which shapes their behavior and expectations from others. When the status quo is disrupted, uncertainty about one's societal position increases. For example, the surge in racial terror lynchings in the United States between 1877 and 1950 coincided with social upheaval following the Civil War, Reconstruction, and the end of chattel slavery, threatening established racial norms.

In response to such uncertainty, individuals may turn to extremist ideologies or groups, which validate perceived threats and offer belonging, status, and agency (Strindberg, 2020). Thus, uncertainty can push individuals toward extremism, while group identification provides a stabilizing pull.

Both the staircase model and SIT address the psychological and situational factors shaping identity and self-perception. Although contemporary radicalization theories recognize the importance of both individual and environmental factors, they often overemphasize the role of group identity, failing to adequately explain lone actor violence and self-radicalization without group involvement.

2.2.6 Social-Psychology and Self-Radicalization

The surge in studies on leaderless resistance, jihad, self-radicalization, and lone-actor violence reflects the growing influence of social media in society (Thompson, 2011; von Behr et al., 2013; Hamm and Spaaij, 2017; McDowell-Smith et al., 2017; Johnson, 2018; Fisogni, 2019; Vacca, 2019; Hartleb, 2020; Hollewell and Longpre, 2022).

Internet radicalization is not new, but its role has shifted. Previously, the Web was used mainly for planning and secret communication in password-protected forums. While these forums also spread propaganda, their influence was limited compared to today. Now, extremist groups exploit social media's core function – building networks – to spread their ideology.

The emergence of online extremist networks has reduced the necessity for in-person group contact to engage in extremist activities. Kruglanski and colleagues (2018, 2019, 2020; Webber et al., 2018) explore this through a social-psychological lens, theorizing that an individual's quest for personal significance is a key motivator. They term this drive the Quest for Significance Theory (QST), which posits that people universally seek recognition and value from others (Webber et al., 2018; Kruglanski et al., 2019, 2022b).

QST is based on three components: The Need, The Narrative, and The Network (Kruglanski et al., 2019, 2022b). The Need represents the push factor, driven by a desire for personal significance. This need can be triggered by a loss of significance, the anticipation of such a loss, or the opportunity for significance gain (Kruglanski et al., 2019, 2022b).

The Narrative serves as the pull factor, linking the quest for significance to extremist actions. While the need alone doesn't lead to extremism, when a group's ideology convinces an individual that violence will fulfill their significance need, the narrative justifies their actions (Kruglanski et al., 2019, 2022b).

The final component, The Network, is crucial for spreading the ideological narrative and activating the need for significance. Traditionally, social networks have played a key role in recruitment and indoctrination. Social connections, especially with trusted friends and family, reduce resistance to extremist narratives (Chaiken et al., 1996; Cialdini and Goldstein, 2004; Sageman, 2004, 2008).

With the advent of the internet and social media, one's social network has evolved beyond that of purely face-to-face interactions. "Exposure to charismatic leaders and persuasive communicators in Internet chat rooms, via propaganda videos ... are also part of the process" (Kruglanski et al., 2019, pp. 51–52). Consequently, no matter if one's social network is entirely in-person, entirely online, or a combination of both, an individual's social network today is much more dynamic, thereby providing more opportunities for extremist and terrorist groups to reach their target audience.

QST (Kruglanski et al., 2019, 2022b) provides a guiding framework for this study because it accounts for both group contact radicalization and self-radicalization; and it acknowledges that while social conditions are crucial to one's psychological perspective, that one's psychologically driven personal need for significance within society is not a sufficient motivator. Extremist behavior requires the existence of a social network, as well as exposure to the appropriate ideological narrative by way of this network.

2.2.7 Social Neuroscience Explanations

Social neuroscience is an interdisciplinary field that employs neuroscientific techniques to study how social processes influence behavior, thoughts, and emotions (Ito and Kubota, 2023, 2024). It is commonly understood as the study of social psychology topics through a multilevel perspective, incorporating brain and body analysis (Ito and Kubota, 2023).

This field assumes specific brain regions correspond to psychological processes, enabling the use of neuroscience tools like EEG to explore psychological variables and their interactions. Social neuroscience contributes to the radicalization literature by providing both a methodological approach and a theoretical framework. In addition, advances in technology have made brain studies more cost-effective, allowing researchers to address previously unanswered questions.

Victoroff (2005) was among the first to advocate for a brain-behavior approach to studying radicalization, terrorism, and extremism, criticizing traditional fields for failing to develop comprehensive models due to their narrow, top-down analyses (Husna, 2020). More recent studies emphasize the need to integrate neural-psychological processes with social, political, and economic factors to fully understand radicalization (Decety and Workman, 2017; Decety and Yoder, 2017; Hamid, 2019; Husna, 2020; Shafi, 2021). Social neuroscience addresses these issues by examining the interplay between neural mechanisms and the social and environmental contexts that shape behavior.

Through longitudinal analysis and neuroimaging, social neuroscience research on radicalization shows that when situational stressors converge with individual traits like justice sensitivity, anomalous genetic expressions and predisposition, cognitive inflexibility, or cognitive closure, then extremist violence is a likely outcome (Yoder and Decety, 2014; Decety and Yoder, 2016, 2017; Zmigrod et al., 2019).

Justice sensitivity is a trait emotion that indicates how an individual processes issues of justice as they observe and encounter them in their daily lives. In an effort to understand the neural process involved in justice sensitivity, several studies determined that for individuals who perceive that a personal and/or intragroup injustice has occurred, this injustice will trigger a response of anger, which can motivate an individual to restore justice through the use of intergroup violence and aggression (Yoder and Decety, 2014; Decety and Yoder, 2016, 2017; Decety and Workman, 2017). This body of research finds that justice sensitivity can be measured in two key regions of the brain – the dorsolateral and dorsomedial prefrontal cortex (dlPFC, dmPFC) and the posterior superior and temporal sulcus (pSTS) (Yoder and Decety, 2014; Decety and Yoder, 2016, 2017; Decety and Workman, 2017). Observing neural activation in these regions of the brain is significant because these areas directly correspond with executive functioning, which is responsible for regulating prosocial behaviors such as empathy, morality, and judgment.

Several studies have established a link between genetic disposition and violence (Alsobrook and Pauls, 2000; Caspi et al., 2002; Ferguson and Beaver, 2009; McDermott et al., 2009; Tubvlad, 2011; Glenn and Rainne, 2014; Garcia-Arocena, 2015; Tihonen et al., 2015). This vein of research indicates that alterations in the expression of certain brain-based genes such as MAO-A, DAT1, and DRS2 can impact specific neurotransmitters, like that of serotonin, dopamine, and norepinephrine (Krakowski, 2003; McDermott et al., 2009; Crockett et al., 2010). This is a key connection because neurotransmitters are essential to the processing of human emotion, aggression, and cognition.

One of the most significant findings to date regarding the relationship between genetics and violence has been that of the *warrior gene*. Monoamine oxidase A (MAO-A) – the warrior gene – is an enzyme located in the X chromosome (Online Appendix Figures 23 and 24). Abnormal expressions of this gene have been linked to aggression in human beings; and deficient activity of this gene places an individual at a higher risk for violence if they have also been exposed to childhood trauma (Caspi et al., 2002; Klasen et al., 2018).

It is important to highlight the latter finding regarding the environmental impact of childhood trauma because it underscores the key role that environmental factors play in this dynamic. Decades of research indicate that while the genetic contribution to violent behavior is approximately 50 percent, environmental factors – which broadly captures one's physical environment as well as social interactions – account for the remaining 50 percent (Alsobrook and Pauls, 2000; Garcia-Arocena, 2015). While genetic disposition is important, one's environment can mediate or exacerbate the expression of the genes that contribute to violent and aggressive behaviors (Baker et al., 2008; Bezdjian et al., 2011; Tuvblad and Baker, 2011; Reiss et al., 2013).

Though our understanding of cognitive (in)flexibility has its origins in cognitive psychology, social neuroscience has contributed greatly to this research perspective by allowing researchers to measure this neural process using brain imaging. Therefore, social neuroscience allows us to move beyond self-report scale measures which are subject to biases and validity challenges, and instead objectively capture whether an individual exhibits this cognitive trait.

Cognitive flexibility is an executive function that represents one's mental capacity to shift between two discrete concepts, as well as their ability to comprehend and synthesize multiple concepts simultaneously (Husna, 2020). As an executive function, cognitive flexibility is observed in the prefrontal cortex (PFC) region of the brain, specifically that of the dorsolateral prefrontal cortex (dlPFC) and the orbitofrontal cortex (OFC). In early animal studies it was determined that cognitive flexibility is essential to animal survival, because it is what allows an animal to adapt its behavior in response to an evolving situation (Müller and Pillay, 2024). Similarly, human beings require cognitive flexibility in order to adapt to new environments, people, and situational stressors. When this executive function is diminished, an individual has a much higher likelihood of struggling to adjust to new situations, disruptions to their routine, and even evolving societal changes. What that translates to behaviorally is that this person is less tolerant in their views, can possess a rigid mindset that is not readily adaptable, has difficulty recognizing nuance, and can be irrational in debates and negotiations. Given the individual traits of cognitive inflexibility (i.e. low levels of cognitive flexibility), Decety and Workman (2017) assert that these individuals are more susceptible to extremist messaging than the average person, because they see the world in black and white, and once they've embraced a specific ideological message, they are unable to consider alternative viewpoints.

Cognitive closure is often discussed within the context of cognitive (in)flexibility, because the two processes tend to function together, and if an individual exhibits cognitive inflexibility, then they will generally also exhibit cognitive closure (Zhong et al., 2017). By extension, evidence of cognitive closure is also captured by neuroimaging of the dorsolateral prefrontal cortex (dlPFC) and the orbitofrontal cortex (OFC) regions of the brain. Cognitive closure can be described as one's need to have a definitive answer on any given topic, and an aversion to ambiguity (Husna, 2020). A person who suffers from cognitive closure will demonstrate an unwillingness to have their personal beliefs, knowledge, and views challenged and will reject opposite viewpoints even in the face of evidence.

DeZavala et al. find that individuals who possess a conservative worldview, when coupled with cognitive closure, have higher levels of out-group hostility and view intergroup relations as a source of conflict, in comparison to a person who is cognitively open (2010). Intergroup differentiation is considered one of the main precursors to extremism because it contributes to out-group hostility, and cognitive closure reinforces intergroup differentiation (Obaidi et al., 2023). Further, when cognitive closure and cognitive inflexibility operate together, there is the increased risk that this individual will adopt extremist views and exhibit extremist behavior (Zmigrod et al., 2019; Zmigrod, 2020; Schumann, et al., 2022). For example, Zmigrod et al. find that the more rigid and inflexible one's cognitive disposition, the greater one's willingness to engage in violence, or even die, in defense of one's national in-group against perceived out-group threats (2019).

The contribution of social neuroscience to the literatures on radicalization and extremism cannot be overstated. As a result of this field of study and methodological approach, we now have biological indicators of radicalization risk, as well as one's risk for extremist violence, that can be measured using brain imaging devices and other instrumentation techniques that simultaneously capture physiological responses. Therefore, we now have the capacity to move beyond inferences and observe psychosomatic indicators of a radicalized mindset and one's vulnerability to extremist ideology.

2.2.8 Social Psychology, Social Neuroscience, and the Key Role of Empathy

Social psychology and social neuroscience have collectively made great strides to advance brain–behavior perspectives on radicalization and violent extremism, and this is evident given the research on the psychological process of empathy, how it is influenced by situational conditions, and its connection to extremist ideation and behaviors.

When one thinks of empathy, the word is more than likely associated with altruism and prosocial behavior. However, both social psychologists and social neuroscientists have been instrumental in deconstructing the nuances of empathy and highlighting the role it plays in the radicalization process. Experimental evidence demonstrates that high levels of in-group empathy can actually have an inverse effect on the levels of empathy for an out-group. Specifically, "if people feel the suffering of in-group members particularly acutely, this may motivate them to act against members of an out-group that they see as responsible" (Bruneau, 2016, p. 9).

Cognitive neuroscientist,[1] Emile Bruneau explains that:

> The more empathy participants reported feeling for the suffering of random out-group members, the greater their willingness to help and the less their willingness to harm needy members of that group. However, empathy for in-group suffering predicted the opposite: less willingness to help the out-group and more willingness to harm. In fact, this is the conclusion drawn by a number of researchers who have interviewed attempted suicide bombers or families of people who engaged in suicide bombings. Although, some who commit political violence appear to be unhampered by empathy, the majority tend to be characterized by a strong [empathetic] communal focus ... (2016, p. 9)

Bruneau describes empathy as an internal tug-of-war, whereby the stronger the level of empathy for the in-group, and the weaker the level of empathy for the out-group, the more likely a person is to endorse and engage in intergroup violence.

Consequently, it is not just one's capacity for empathy that is important, but also the recipient (out-group vs. in-group) of one's empathy and the difference

---

[1] Cognitive psychology is an adjacent sub-field to both social neuroscience and social psychology that explores the connections between cognitive psychology and neuroscience.

between the levels of empathy toward both the out-group and in-group that best predicts whether a person will engage in extremism.

Empathy is central to the core argument presented in this Element, not only because it is a predictor of extremism, but because it also functions as a protective mechanism. In the 2015 study by Feddes et al., the authors investigate the impact of empathy on violent radicalization over time (2015). The authors incorporate several additional factors in their analysis, including individual and collective deprivation, as well as social disconnectedness, which measure the subjects' feelings of connectedness to their neighborhood and their country of residence. The findings of this study indicate that prior to the intervention event, which was a series of trainings to encourage out-group empathy and perspective taking, the participants reported statistically significant lower levels of out-group empathy, and statistically significant higher levels of support for violent radicalization, in comparison to the outcome measures post-intervention (Feddes et al., 2015). Interestingly, the study did not find evidence that collective deprivation, individual deprivation, or social disconnectedness have any impact on violent radicalization, at either the pre-intervention stage or the post-intervention stage.

The importance of the Bruneau (2016) and the Feddes et al. (2015) studies is twofold. First, we now understand that empathy can promote prosocial behavior that decreases out-group hostility and support for violent radicalization. However, the second point that is equally critical is that when in-group empathy is significantly higher than empathy for the out-group that this disparity can encourage feelings of othering and out-group dehumanization, which is the basis for violent radicalization and extremism. In Section 3, I explore this dynamic further and build upon this premise, which grounds the theoretical foundation of this study.

2.3 Radicalization: The Outcomes – from Radicalism to Hate Crimes

Terms like radicalism, extremism, fundamentalism, terrorism, and hate crimes are often contested, poorly defined, and used interchangeably, thereby complicating the study of specific phenomena. Rather than aiming to define these concepts universally, my goal is to create an operational framework to analyze the neural and psychological effects of online propaganda videos produced or endorsed by terrorists and extremists, and to assess the potential for violence stemming from these effects. This requires a careful examination of these terms within the context of existing literature on radicalization and political violence.

Historically, radicalism referred to efforts to transform societal structures but has recently been narrowed to describe intolerant attitudes that reject democratic values (Rieger et al., 2013; Maskaliūnaitė, 2015). Fundamentalism, often linked to religious ideology, denotes rigid, uncompromising beliefs but can also apply to strict political views. Despite their differences, both radicalism and fundamentalism share the characteristic that individuals can hold these beliefs without resorting to violence (McCauley and Moskalenko, 2011). Some scholars argue that radicalism has historically been more aligned with activism (Pisiou, 2012), while fundamentalism is an anti-modern, anti-liberal mentality that rarely leads to violence (Carpenter, 1997; Maskaliūnaitė, 2015). In contrast, extremism and terrorism are generally associated with political violence, whereas hate crimes, while sharing some overlap, have notable distinctions that will be discussed.

The *Oxford Dictionary of English* defines an "extremist" as someone holding extreme political or religious views (2010, p. 621). This definition is problematic because it frames extremism as relative and needing a comparison category. Scholars often characterize extremism as attitudes and behaviors outside societal norms, which are also described as nonnormative beliefs and actions (Tausch et al., 2011; Neuman, 2013; Schmid, 2013). However, this definition is context-dependent and reflects temporal social constructions.

The term "extremism" is intentionally vague and fluid. Scholars have avoided value-based definitions, preferring a broad term that encompasses both actions and beliefs (McCauley and Moskalenko, 2010; Neuman, 2013; Maskaliūnaitė, 2015). This approach acknowledges that individuals can hold extreme beliefs without engaging in extreme actions (McCauley and Moskalenko, 2010; Neumann, 2013; Khalil et al., 2022; Clever et al., 2023). Wintrobe (2012) highlights this complexity by classifying extremism into three categories: those with extreme beliefs but no extreme actions, those with both, and those with nonextremist beliefs who use extreme means. This framework suggests extremism can be violent or nonviolent, a distinction some scholars find crucial (Geelhoed, 2011; Knight et al., 2017, 2019).

Clever et al. (2023) closely link extremism with radicalism, emphasizing that extremism itself is not inherently violent. They argue for distinguishing extremism (acceptance of violence for a radical ideology) from violent extremism (execution of ideologically motivated violence) (Khalil et al., 2022; Clever et al., 2023). However, other scholars argue that distinguishing between "functional and doctrinal extremism" risks equating violent extremism too closely with terrorism, which they see as problematic (Winter et al., 2020).

Maskaliūnaitė (2015) challenges the necessity of distinguishing violent from nonviolent extremism, criticizing countering violent extremism (CVE) programs for creating a breeding ground for terrorism by making this distinction. Instead, he views all forms of extremism as concerning for opposing democratic norms, human rights, equality, and tolerance.

In this study, I adopt Alex Schmid's definition of extremism, which is broad enough to encompass both ideation and action but also precise enough to guide analysis. Schmid defines extremism as a drive to create a homogeneous society based on rigid, dogmatic ideologies, seeking conformity by suppressing opposition and subjugating minorities (2013, p. 9). This definition distinguishes extremism from radicalism and fundamentalism, which, while promoting rigid and intolerant beliefs, do not explicitly seek societal homogeneity or minority subjugation. Therefore, while radicalism and fundamentalism contain extremist elements, they lack the ideological intensity of extremism as defined here.

Schmid's definition of extremism is largely consistent with other interpretations of the term in that those who adopt extremist ideologies desire a homogeneous society, along parameters defined by their beliefs. For some extremists, for example, white extremists, societal homogeneity can only be achieved by marginalizing and repressing minorities (i.e. race, ethnicity, religion, national origin, sexual orientation, gender, disability, etc.) in society. Thus, while there is the recognition that not all extremist actions represent a hate crime, the basis for criminal hate speech, harassment, and violence is rooted in extremist ideology.

In her analysis of hate crime, Jennifer Schweppe describes a hate crime as "a phenomenon that reaches across the spectrum of hostilities that are manifested towards minority communities, ranging from criminal acts, to discrimination, to hate speech, to microaggressions" (2021, p. 1). And while victimization can occur both in-person and online as two distinct and separate phenomena, a growing body of research shows that the use of criminal hate speech on the internet is highly correlated with in-person hate crimes (Relia et al., 2019; William et al., 2020; Leitch and Pickering, 2022; Lupu et al., 2023; Stremlau et al., 2024).

In a recent NYU study of 532 million tweets published between 2011 and 2016, the authors find that despite variations in city type and size, that as the number of targeted and discriminatory tweets increased in a city, so did the number of hate crimes (Relia et al., 2019). Studies in the UK have come to similar conclusions, finding that there is a correlation between online hate speech and physical hate crime (William et al., 2020; Ofcom and Traverse 2023).

Research into online criminal hate speech and harassment also indicates that victims experience psychological harm and trauma, suicidal ideation, and adverse economic impact due to missed days and lost wages (Saha et al., 2019; Petrosyan, 2022; Dreißigacker et al., 2024). One study determined that nearly half (44 percent) of the survey respondents were negatively impacted (mentally, emotionally and/or financially) by targeted online criminal hate speech (Petrosyan, 2022).

While my working definition of extremism includes physical hate crimes, it's crucial to recognize the impact of so-called "nonviolent extremists." These individuals not only cause harm through online hate crimes but often progress to violent extremism, motivated by beliefs that endorse the subjugation or eradication of minority groups. As such, Schmid's flexible definition of extremism accommodates both physical and online hate crimes.

Terrorism, unlike radicalism, fundamentalism, extremism, or hate crime, is not an ideological belief system but a tactic. It can be used to advance any of these phenomena and is often defined by the scale of the attack and the type of target (Howard, 2010a). This has led to disagreements about what constitutes terrorism (Hoffman, 2006).

The debate over what qualifies as terrorism versus legitimate resistance has long divided scholars (Rapoport, 2022; Hoffman, 2006). The term "terrorism" is inherently subjective, often reflecting the user's moral stance. Sympathy for the victim typically leads to labeling an act as terrorism, while sympathy for the perpetrator may lead to the opposite conclusion. Thus, consensus on its definition is unlikely, except for the general agreement that terrorism is a subjective term.

Despite variations, most scholarly definitions of terrorism include two key elements: it involves violence or the threat of violence against noncombatants, and it aims to intimidate or compel a population, government, or organization into a desired course of action (Maogoto, 2003). Some definitions focus on the perpetrator's characteristics, motivations, and methods (Ganor, 2002), or consider premeditation and property destruction (Winkates, 2006). However, these nuances complicate the distinction between terrorism and other forms of political violence, such as hate crime and extremism.

This study adopts the Australian government's legislative definition of terrorism, which, like Schmid's definition of extremism, is comprehensive, yet detailed enough to distinguish it from other types of political violence:

> As outlined in S100.1, Part 5.3 of Australia's Criminal Code Act 1995 (Cth): [terrorism is defined as] an action or threat of action that causes serious physical harm or death to a person, or endangers a person's life or involves serious risk to public health or safety, serious damage to property or serious interference with essential electronic systems ... It is an action or threat of action intended to advance a political, ideological or religious cause and to

> coerce or influence by intimidation the [U.S.] or [a] foreign government or intimidate the public or a section of the public. (Nasser-Eddine, 2011, p. 7)

Although it is quite detailed, this definition is consistent with the larger body of literature that characterizes terrorism as an action or the threat of action. Thus, terrorism still represents a tactic that can be used by radicals, fundamentalists, and/or extremists to advance their specific ideological, religious, or political goals. Hate crime is notably absent from the aforementioned list, not because those who commit hate crimes don't use terrorism as a tactic, but mainly because in this study, hate crime is encompassed within the conceptualization of extremism, since I argue it is more ideologically aligned with extremism than terrorism. And in a study on the relationship between hate crime and terrorism, the authors arrive at a similar conclusion (Deloughery et al., 2012).

They argue that if one focuses on the characteristics of the perpetrator and victim(s), that terrorism is more often considered an "upward crime," where the perpetrator occupies a lower social class than the victim(s); whereas, a hate crime is a "downward crime" where the perpetrator tends to belong to the majority or dominant group in society while the victim(s) tends to belong to the minority group (Deloughery et al., 2012). Also, the authors do not find any evidence that hate crimes are a precursor to future acts of terrorism, and that it is actually the opposite – hate crimes more often occur in retaliatory response to a terrorist attack (Deloughery et al., 2012).

Although, in this study, I do not define terrorism according to the victim–perpetrator dynamic, the findings of Deloughery et al.'s research suggest that terrorism and hate crime are two distinct phenomena, with divergent political and ideological goals (2012). So, while I admit there are examples of incidents that *could* be classified as both a hate crime and terrorism, they overwhelmingly are not classified as both due to prosecutorial decisions that take into account conviction rates and sentencing and because the prevailing argument is that hate crimes are not committed to advance a specific political goal, or achieve some tangible concession, consequently, there is little basis to view them as aligned or overlapping with terrorism.

Just as there are parallels between extremism and hate crime, I recognize there is also overlap between violent extremism and terrorism (Table 3). That is because violent extremism can also represent an act of terrorism when the violence undertaken is to advance a specific religious, political, or ideological cause or achieve a tangible goal.

For example, the violent campaign of ISIS/ISIL between 2014 and 2016 that involved the targeted killings of Coptic and Assyrian Christians, Westerners, and Shia Muslims in order to advance the group's aim of creating an Islamic

Table 3 Definitional approaches to "violent extremism" that reference terrorism[a]

Governmental

Australia (1*): "Violent extremism is the beliefs and actions of people who support or use violence to achieve ideological, religious or political goals. This includes terrorism and other forms of politically motivated and communal violence."

Canada (2*): "[V]iolent extremism" is where an offense is "primarily motivated by extreme political, religious or ideological views." Some definitions explicitly note that radical views are by no means a problem in themselves, but that they become a threat to national security when such views are put into violent action

USA (3*): The FBI defines violent extremism as the "encouraging, condoning, justifying, or supporting the commission of a violent act to achieve political, ideological, religious, social, or economic goals," while USAID defines violent extremist activities as the "advocating, engaging in, preparing, or otherwise supporting ideologically motivated or justified violence to further social, economic or political objectives."

Norway (4*): Violent extremism constitutes activities of persons and groups that are willing to use violence in order to achieve political, ideological or religious goals.

Sweden (5*): A violent extremist is someone "deemed repeatedly to have displayed behavior that does not just accept the use of violence but also supports or exercises ideologically motivated violence to promote something."

UK (6*): Extremism is defined as the vocal or active opposition to fundamental values, including democracy, the rule of law, individual liberty and the mutual respect and tolerance of different faiths and beliefs, as well as calls for the death of United Kingdom armed forces at home or abroad.

Intergovernmental

Organization for Economic Cooperation and Development (OECD) (7*): "[P]romoting views which foment and incite violence in furtherance of particular beliefs, and foster hatred which might lead to inter-community violence"

United Nations Educational, Scientific and Cultural Organization (UNESCO) (8*): While recognizing that there is no internationally agreed-upon definition, UNESCO, within the *Preventing Violent Extremism through Education: A Guide for Policy-makers* document, suggested that the most common understanding of the term, and the one which it follows within the guide, is one that "refers to the beliefs and actions of people who support or use violence to

Table 3 (cont.)

Intergovernmental

---

achieve ideological, religious or political goals." This can include "**terrorism and other forms of politically motivated violence.**"

---

[a] United Nations Office on Drugs and Crime (UNODC). (2018). "Counter-Terrorism Module Two-Key Issues: Radicalization and Violent Extremism." www.unodc.org/e4j/zh/terrorism/module-2/key-issues/radicalization-violent-extremism.html.

1* Parliament of Australia (2015). "Australian Government measures to counter violent extremism: a quick guide." February.

2* Public Safety Canada (2009). "Assessing the Risk of Violent Extremists." Research Summary, vol. 14, no. 4.

3* USAID (2011). " The Development Response to Violent Extremism and Insurgency: Putting Principles Into Practice." USAID Policy, September 2011. P. 2.

4* Norwegian Ministry of Justice and Public Security (2014). " Action Plan Against Radicalization and Violent Extremism." P.7.

5* Government Offices of Sweden (2011). " Sweden Action Plan to Safeguard Democracy Against Violence Promoting Extremism." Government Communication 2011/12:44, Point 3.2.

6* HM Government (UK) (2015). Counter-Extremism Strategy. London, Counter-Extremism Directorate, Home Office. Para. 1. See too HM Government (2011). Prevent Strategy. The Stationery Office, Norwich. Annex A. Note that the 2013 UK Task Force on Tackling Radicalization and Extremism defined "Islamist extremism."

7* Organization for Economic Cooperation and Development (OECD), Development Assistance Committee (2016). DAC High Level Meeting, Communiqué of February 19, 2016.

State is illustrative of both violent extremism and terrorism. However, this example is a unique one. Despite the definitions presented in Table 3, in practice, most acts of violent extremism do not advance a specific political cause or seek to achieve a specific political aim (Barkun, 1990; Lee and Simms, 2008).

That is because extremism (violent and nonviolent) is primarily ideological and driven by millenarian goals; whereas, terrorism can be driven by ideology, but also by politics or religion, with goals that are explicitly political and tangible, even if they are not always feasible or attainable (i.e. 1988 Hamas Covenant states one of its main goals is the destruction of Israel).[2]

---

[2] "The Covenant of the Hamas-Main Points." (1988). *Charter of Hamas.* https://irp.fas.org/world/para/docs/880818a.htm.

2.4 Key Takeaways from a Review of the Literature

From the discussion of the various forms of political violence it should be more apparent that there are two distinct types that emerge from radicalization: extremism and terrorism. And the following statements echo what has been observed globally over the past decade.

In the United States alone, "white supremacists and right-wing extremists [i.e. the alt-right] are the most significant domestic terrorism threat facing the [nation]."[3] And more generally, across Western nations, far-right extremism has increased 320 percent over the past five years and is the most significant [terrorism] threat facing the West.[4] Meanwhile, for more than two decades, radical Islamic extremism[5] and terrorism[6] continue to be the most significant global terrorism threat.

In 2021, the Islamic State (IS) displaced the Taliban as the deadliest terrorist group in the world, reporting an average of 15.2 deaths per attack. While nearly half (48 percent) of all global terrorism deaths occurred in the Sahel region of sub-Saharan Africa – and all of these attacks were committed by radical Islamic extremist and terrorist groups. Finally, the six most active and lethal terrorist organizations in the world espouse a religious ideology of radical Islamic extremism (Online Appendix Table 18).

Thus, to conclude this section, the two most significant political violence threats facing the world today are right-wing (i.e. alt-right) extremism and radical Islamic terrorism. That is why understanding the internet-based propaganda tools which are presently used by right-wing extremists and radical Islamic terrorists to radicalize an individual is a crucial endeavor, and this is specifically what I explore in the sections that follow.

3 Theoretical Framework

The internet has increasingly become instrumental to the radicalization process. In a study published by the PIRUS (The Profiles of Individual Radicalization in

---

[3] "Domestic Terrorism Prevention Act of 2019." (2019). *U.S. Senate Bill S.894. U.S. Senate, 116th Congress, 1st Session*. www.congress.gov/116/bills/s894/BILLS-116s894is.xml.

[4] "Far-Right Terrorism Increase in the West Explained." (2021). *Institute for Economics & Peace*. September 7. www.visionofhumanity.org/explainer-far-right-terrorism-in-the-west/.

[5] Radical Islamic extremism refers to the beliefs and actions of lone actor terrorists who espouse an Islamic extremism ideology, but who are not affiliated with a specific organization, or acting to directly advance the interests of a specific group. The 2016 Orlando (U.S.) nightclub attack is an example of Islamic extremism. See www.cnn.com/2016/06/12/us/orlando-nightclub-shooting/index.html; www.cbc.ca/news/world/florida-pulse-nightclub-aftermath-1.3632272.

[6] Radical Islamic terrorism refers to the coordinated actions taken by members of organized groups espousing Islamic extremist ideology. The 2015 *Charlie Hebdo* attack in Paris (France) is an example of Radical Islamic terrorism.

the United States) research team, the authors find that between 2005 and 2010, social media played a primary role in the radicalization process for less than 2 percent (1.67 percent) of the study cases (Jensen et al., 2015, 2018). Whereas, between 2011 and 2016, the authors determined that social media played a primary role in the radicalization process for nearly 17 percent (16.95 percent) of the study cases (Jensen et al., 2015, 2018). And "in 2016 alone, social media played some role (whether it was primary or secondary)[7] in the radicalization processes of nearly 90 percent of the extremists in the PIRUS dataset" (Jensen et al., 2018, p. 1). The results of the PIRUS study overlap with those of the International Center for Counter-Terrorism (ICCT), which finds that the sharp increase in the number of lone actor attacks (from just under 5 percent in the mid-1970s to more than 70 percent, between 2014 and 2018) is overwhelmingly a function of the increased rate of radicalization via the internet (Zeiger and Gyte, 2021).

Given the growing body of research on the relationship between the internet and radicalization, it is of crucial importance to work to understand the various modes of internet radicalization, the nature of what is being transmitted between the extremist organization and the radical sympathizer, and the salient types of extremist content. In addition, it is equally important to gain insight into the individual receiver of these radical messages and extremist content to better grasp the neural psychology of the radicalization process.

That is why in this section I build upon the foundational literature discussed in Section 2 to construct a theoretical framework, and work to further elucidate the proposed relationship between empathy, extremist messaging, and online radicalization.

3.1 Radicalization and the Internet

The internet is a murky place, and the radicalization process is one that is complex. So, it is challenging to pinpoint specific features of the internet that are responsible for radicalizing every individual, but in general there are certain tools used consistently on the internet that feature prominently in the radicalization process (Cozma, 2014), which include:

---

[7] "We determined social media as playing a primary role in the radicalization of individuals if their exposure to extremist ideologies and 50% or more of their socialization within extremist movements took place on social media platforms. Similarly, we determined social media as playing a secondary role in the radicalization of U.S. extremists if social media platforms were used to reaffirm or advance pre-existing extremist beliefs that were first acquired through face-to-face relationships. Finally, individuals were coded 'No' for the influence of social media on their radicalization if they were present on social media sites but there is no indication that those sites contributed to their radicalization or mobilization," PIRUS, 2018, p. 2.

1. Watching *propaganda videos* that espouse a specific extremist ideology by (a) glorifying the actions of the terrorist organization or groups, (b) disseminating an extremist message that is meant to resonate with viewers, and/or (c) highlighting the grievances or victimization of the people the extremist group was founded to 'speak' for.

2. Viewing and participating in discussions in specific *chatrooms, forums and on social networking websites*, where propaganda materials are disseminated and issues are discussed, from the narrow lens of the participants (e.g., Stormfront). The social networking features of these websites foster communication and relationship building to such an extent that users feel connected and integrated into the larger movement, even though all of the interaction is online.

3. Participation in *multiplayer and massively multiplayer online games* (*MOG and MMOG*), is yet another emerging frontier in internet-based self-radicalization, as the internet evolves once again. Within the last six-years (since 2018), extremist and terrorist groups have been exploiting the terrain of multiplayer online games to recruit and radicalize individuals. These platforms allow users to post manifestos, learn how to carry out attacks, and "draw inspiration from [the violence] of video game aesthetics."[8] Essentially, extremists use MOG/MMOGs much like they have used social networking websites and chat forums; the main difference is that these online games allow for secure and private communication in real time.

3.1.1 Radicalization, the Internet, and the Role of Empathy

To begin to understand why online radicalization is on the rise, it is important to first understand what is happening to a person when they consume extremist materials on the internet. To do this, I draw upon the research of Kruglanski et al. (2019, 2022b), and the authors' 3 N Model – the Need, the Narrative, and the Network.

Building upon the work of Kruglanski et al. (2019, 2022b), I utilize their framework of the Need, the Narrative, and the Network, while also deviating from their assertions on one key point, and that is their argument regarding one's individual need for personal significance.

According to Kruglanski et al. (2019, 2022b), one's need for personal significance is ego-driven, and while I acknowledge that ego-driven desires are important, and can serve as instigating factors, at the time of this writing, empirical tests of the

---

[8] *Fighting extremism in gaming platforms: A set of design principles to develop comprehensive P/CVE strategies.* (n.d.). International Centre for Counter-Terrorism – ICCT. Retrieved October 8, 2023, from www.icct.nl/publication/fighting-extremism-gaming-platforms-set-design-principles-develop-comprehensive-pcve.

relationship between the ego-driven need for personal significance and radicalization indicate that it is a weak relationship, at best (Da Silva, 2024).

On the other hand, there are a number of studies that have determined that the radicalization process is more often triggered and sustained by strong affective emotions (Davis, 1983, Jasper and Poulsen, 1995; Jasper, 1998; Buckels and Trapnell, 2013; Matsumoto et al., 2015), which are enduring emotions, such as love, hatred, and loyalty. Consequently, one's ego is the psychological manifestation of one's personal identity, and negative challenges to one's personal identity will often produce a confluence of emotions – strong affective emotions – and those emotions are what drive one's need, even the need for personal significance. That is why I argue that the ego-driven need for personal significance is insufficient to set an individual on the radicalization pathway and sustain that person with enough fervor to engage in violence.

Intellectually, we know that emotions are crucial to the radicalization process, but the ability to observe and analyze emotional connections has always been limited. However, with more recent advances in brain imaging technology, and the expanding fields of social psychology and social neuroscience, we have been able to not only better understand the role emotions play in the radicalization process, but also identify the nuances of various cognitive-emotive states, which has led us to recognize the importance of empathy to the radicalization process (Feddes et al., 2015; Bruneau, 2016). Yet, despite the fact that we now realize empathy serves as both a risk and a protective factor for extremism, there are very few existing studies that utilize neural observation to analyze the complexity of this relationship.

3.1.2 The Need: Cognitive-Emotive Empathy, the Need to Defend, and the Need to Dehumanize

Emotions are conscious psychological states accompanied by somatic indicators. Some researchers link emotions to feelings (Damasio, 2004; Oosterwijk et al., 2012), while others argue emotions are shaped by social experiences (Johnson-Laird and Oatley, 2000; Turner, 2009). Most agree on two key points: emotions are either affective or reactive, and emotions are tied to cognition, meaning they involve beliefs and can be influenced by thoughts (Jasper, 1998).

Research shows that both affective and reactive emotions are crucial in radical political actions at all stages of an organization's life (Davis, 1983; Jasper and Poulsen, 1995; Jasper, 1998; Buckels and Trapnell, 2013; Matsumoto et al., 2015). Jasper was among the first to theorize that group leaders use affective emotions to recruit and retain members (1998). Affective emotions, such as love, hatred, and loyalty, are enduring, and rooted in belief systems, while reactive

Table 4 Emotions that influence radical political behavior

EMOTIONS

Primarily Affective
Hatred, Hostility, Loathing, Suspicion, Paranoia
Solidarity, Loyalty, Trust, Respect, Love

Primarily Reactive
Anger, Grief, Loss, Sorrow, Outrage, Indignation, Shame

Moods and Intermediary Emotions
Compassion, Sympathy, Pity, Cynicism, Depression
Defiance, Enthusiasm, Pride, Envy, Resentment
Fear, Dread, Joy, Hope, Resignation

Source: Jasper, James. (1998). "The emotions of protest: Affective and reactive emotions in and around social movements."

emotions, like anger and grief, are responses to specific events and are temporary. Jasper identifies these emotions and moods as key influences on radical political behavior, as outlined in Table 4.

Emotions permeate every facet of social interaction. Despite this, every individual who experiences anger, loyalty, fear, or hatred is not motivated to join a terrorist or extremist organization, or carry out an attack. This logic can also be extended to every individual who consumes terrorist or extremist propaganda; not every viewer will be radicalized, not even if the propaganda messages evoke an empathetic response. I argue that this is because the pathway from message exposure to radicalization is heavily influenced by an individual's existing belief system and the capacity to reconcile one's belief system with the propaganda message through the process of empathy. Figure 2 illustrates this process, which I define as the *Cognitive-Emotive Model of Radicalization.*[9]

The Cognitive-Emotive Model of Radicalization is developed based upon the assertion that radical information received by the individual *must generate an empathetic response that is consistent with existing beliefs for the process of radical identification to occur.* I believe the reason why empathy plays such a central role in the recruitment and radicalization of individuals has much to do with how this process evolves within the conscious mind.

Empathy can be categorized along two dimensions: trait empathy and state empathy. When empathy is characterized as a trait, it refers to the "reaction of

---

[9] This model builds upon Geoff Dean's *5.4nitive Model of Radicalization*. See Geoff Dean. (2014). *Neurocognitive Risk Assessment for the Early Detection of Violent Extremists*. Springer Briefs in Criminology.

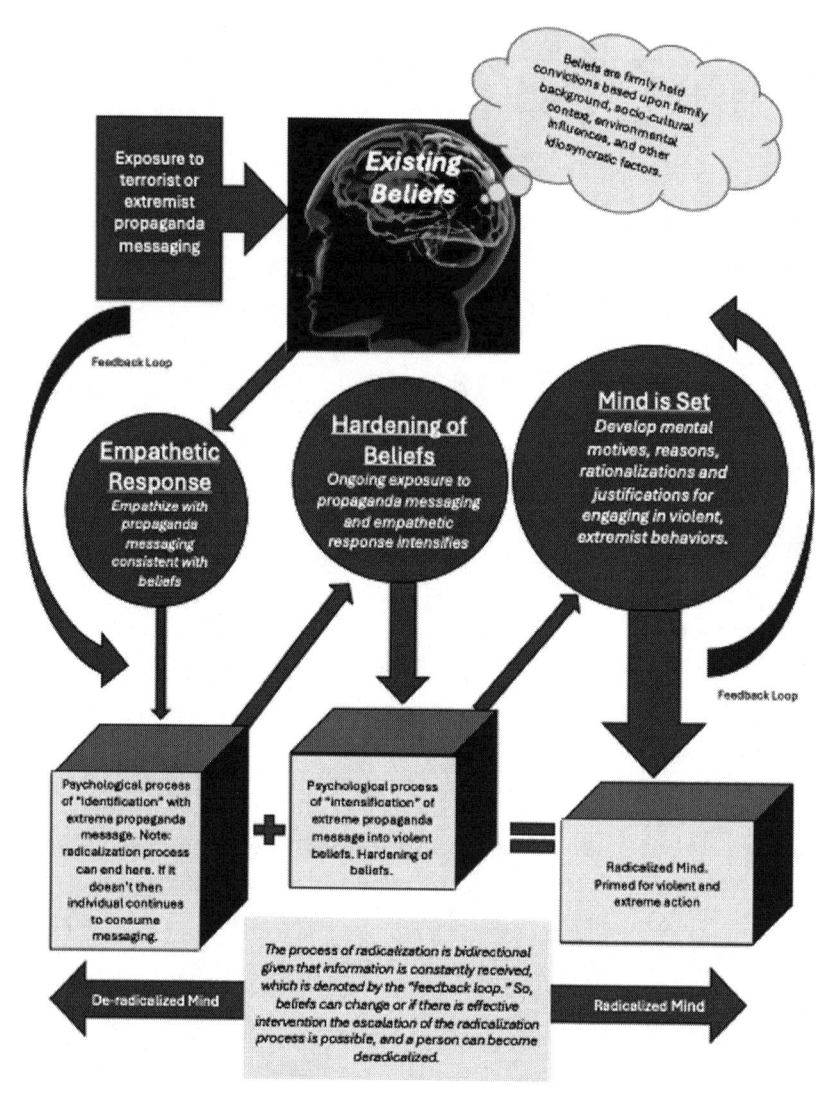

Figure 2 The cognitive-emotive model of radicalization

one individual to the observed experiences of another" (Davis, 1983, p. 114). In this sense, empathy is an emotional trait or feeling that is transitory (Williams, 1990; Zillmann, 2006). Whereas when empathy is characterized as a state of being, it refers to the process by which an individual understands or relates to other individuals or situations (Lazarus, 1991; Shen, 2010).

In this sense, empathy is a cognitive process that "occurs when the attended perception of the object's state (automatically) activates the subject's representations of the state, situation and object, and that activation of these representations automatically primes or generates the associated automatic and somatic responses" (Preston and de Waal, 2002, p. 4). Although, state empathy is conditioned upon the existence or occurrence of trait empathy, researchers have come to agree that empathy is not a monolithic cognitive or affective response that can be reduced to a reactive emotional trait, but rather a dynamic physiological, psychological, and neural process. It is for that reason that the study of trait empathy is not applicable to this analysis.

There is an understanding that state empathy involves the interaction between affective and cognitive functions, as well as the associative process of identification (Bagozzi and Moore, 1994; Preston and de Waal, 2002; Campbell and Babrow, 2004; Chory-Assad and Cicchirillo, 2005). Affective empathy is characterized by an individual's activation and experience of affective reactions to another's expressions of emotions and/or experiences, regardless of whether they are positive or negative emotions, or even multiple contending emotions (Preston and de Waal, 2002; Jabbi et al., 2007). Thus, affective empathy involves the understanding and sharing of another's feelings (Lazarus, 1991; Decety and Jackson, 2006; Smith, 2010).

On the other hand, cognitive empathy refers to the capacity to recognize, comprehend, and adopt another's viewpoint. Cognitive empathy involves perspective taking by psychologically placing oneself in another person's condition or circumstance. Although cognitive and affective empathy are discrete processes, one cannot exist without the other and still be considered empathy. "Shared affect without shared cognition would mean little more than mimicry. Similarly, shared cognition without shared affect would be sympathy, instead of empathy" (Eisenberg and Miller, 1987; Goldie, 1999; Shen, 2010, p. 399).

In the study of empathy, the associative element is often overlooked (Preston and de Waal, 2002), but it is a vital component in the empathetic process, especially as it relates to how individuals interpret and relate to emotionally based messages. The associative element in state empathy is defined by its primary function, which is to facilitate relationship development; and is often characterized as "identification" (Campbell and Babrow, 2004; Chory-Assad and Cicchirillo, 2005). Identification with a message, such as extremist propaganda, is the internal process through which the audience experiences reception and interpretation of the message (Cohen, 2006). From the functional perspective, it is this feature of state empathy that enables relationship development which facilitates the transition from perception (of the message) to action (i.e. acting on the message).

Now there is one notable caveat about the latter statement on the transition from message perception to action that must be accounted for if this process is to occur, and that is the role of persuasion. Media messages, by design, are emotive and can stimulate an empathetic response, but they are not necessarily persuasive. That is because the role of the media is to primarily inform the public with its messaging content (Falk et al., 2010). In a similar fashion, propaganda messages, by design, are persuasive, but they are not necessarily emotive or capable of triggering an empathetic response. That is because persuasive messaging is a form of human communication that is intended to influence the autonomous actions and judgments of individuals; which can be achieved using techniques such as logic and reasoning. For example, advertising commercials often appeal to one's logic and reason by convincing the audience of their need for a certain product without ever triggering an emotional response (Falk et al., 2010).

However, when it comes to extremist messaging, for it to be effective in facilitating the transition from message perception to tangible action, the message must trigger a sustained emotional empathetic response over multiple settings that is consistent with one's beliefs; but for it to be persuasive, it must also utilize propaganda devices in the conveyance of its ideological message (Shen, 2014).

In sum, empathetic responses to emotive persuasive messaging function on a continuum. There exist intermediate stages of empathy in message processing that oscillate between empathic arousal and the complete internalization of the message and its advocacy. After initial exposure, the intensity and duration of a message's influence is then determined by an individual's existing belief system and the continued exposure to similarly themed messages.

This explains how empathetic responses can be stimulated in an experimental setting (i.e. empathetic arousal), which can be observed, but then not lead to radicalization; while outside the experimental setting, message-induced empathetic responses have resulted in the radicalization of individuals.

3.1.3 The Narrative: Extremist Propaganda Messaging and Strategic Narratives, Victim Portrayals, and the Charismatic Leader

Extremist propaganda messaging involves the use of strategic communication by violent extremist and terrorist groups to radicalize, recruit, and mobilize their target audience (Hancock et al., 2010). These groups utilize various digital platforms like social media, web forums, multiplayer video games, and web-based videos to reach members, supporters, and potential recruits (Farwell, 2014; Shane and Hubbard, 2014; Gambhir, 2014; Carr, 2014).

As discussed in Section 3.1, while any of these platforms can serve to radicalize and recruit, web-based videos have distinct advantages due to their ease of production, rapid dissemination, and ability to convey a controlled narrative directly from the organization (Amble, 2012; Allendorfer and Herring, 2015; Cohen et al., 2016).

Propaganda can be broadly defined as "any attempt to persuade to a belief or a form of action" (Hummell and Huntress, 1949, p. 2; Tuttle Ross, 2002, p. 17; Antilla, 2010), the understanding of which is that the goal of propaganda is to influence human behavior. This makes propaganda, both an important style of communication as well as a powerful device, one that inherently relies upon a combination of textual and verbal language cues, sounds, symbols, and imagery to convey its message.

One of the most impactful forms of propaganda utilized by extremist and terrorist groups is that of narratives. Narratives are powerful communication tools. A narrative is "a system of stories that share themes, forms, and archetypes" (Corman, 2011, p. 37). Casebeer and Russell contend that narratives "influence our ability to recall events, motivate people to act, modulate our emotional reactions to events, cue certain heuristics and biases, structure our problem-solving capabilities, and ultimately ... constitute our very identity" (2005, p. 6). Our societal values are embedded within narratives; thus, our response to narratives is primarily emotional, making them inherently persuasive.

Narrative messages have been proposed as an effective tool for overcoming and reducing psychological resistance to persuasion (Wojcieszak and Kim, 2016). In a recent study, Yoder et al. examine heroic and social martyr narratives produced by ISIS within the context of an individual's dominant cognitive disposition of empathy versus egoism (2020). Similar to this research, the authors also use EEG to measure the strength of an individual's reaction to the narrative message. The authors find that "recruitment potential was predicted by self-reported narrative transportation" (Yoder et al., 2020, p. 2). In other words, the findings suggest that narrative messages, specifically those of heroic martyrdom, have the highest recruitment potential, regardless of whether or not an individual's cognitive disposition is dominant egoism or dominant empathy (Yoder et al., 2020). It is highly likely that because the Yoder et al. (2020) study relies upon self-report data to measure one's cognitive disposition of egoism versus empathy, the authors are unable to capture the link between narrative messages and empathy. However, recent communications studies suggest that empathy induced by narrative messages can effectively facilitate persuasion and reduce psychological reactance, simultaneously (Bilandzic and Busselle, 2013; Braddock and Dillard, 2016; Shen, 2019). Thus, building upon this handful of studies, I contend that message induced empathy operates as a specific communication mechanism capable of eliciting empathy in audience members toward the content presented in the narrative, which, in turn, functions as the basis for persuasion and message effects.

Beyond the use of narratives, there are two additional propaganda messaging devices that studies have demonstrated play a key role in the individual radicalization process. The first is that of the charismatic leader or charismatic authority. "Originally formulated by Max Weber, charismatic authority is a form of 'legitimate domination' employed by an individual who is perceived to possess divinely given inspired abilities" (Hofmann and Dawson, 2014, p. 349). Charismatic authority refers to the widely accepted power of an individual to lead and command others stemming from the recognition of the individual's possession of these charismatic leadership qualities. Charismatic authority is essential to the foundational elements of a terrorist or extremist organization's existence. Without an almost messianic influence over their followers, as was the case with Bin Laden and Zarqawi, these organizations would splinter into disorganized and fractionalized sub-units without a cohesive, binding central authority or mission.

By extension, just as a charismatic authority is essential to the existence and durability of an organization, they are equally crucial to the group's messaging. Terrorist and extremist group leaders strategically invoke the persona of a charismatic authority in the presentation of their inflammatory speeches and with their media interviews to mobilize their adherents, and recruit new members.

The third effective propaganda tactic for mobilizing and radicalizing individuals is victim portrayal. Terrorist and extremist organizations use these portrayals to humanize injustice, creating diagnostic frames that elicit outrage against perpetrators. By vividly displaying blood, pain, and destruction, victim portrayals invoke strong emotions of anger and outrage, particularly among those who identify with the victims. The power of moral outrage in radicalization is well-documented (Benford and Snow, 2000; Sageman, 2004, 2008). Thus, victim portrayals are potent tools for generating sympathy and empathy, and reducing psychological resistance to engaging in political violence.

3.1.4 The Network: The Use of Internet Technologies by Right-Wing Extremists and Islamic Terrorists to Radicalize and Recruit

As of 2024, global internet penetration has reached 5.35 billion people, which is roughly 66 percent of the world's population.[10] With billions of people using the internet every day, it has become central to global communications and interactions; and terrorist and extremist groups have readily taken advantage of the various platforms across the internet to radicalize, recruit, and communicate (Zeiger and Gyte, 2021). The internet has also allowed individuals with similar

---

[10] *Digital around the World – DataReportal – Global Digital Insights.* (n.d.). DataReportal – Global Digital Insights. https://datareportal.com/global-digital-overview.

beliefs, interests, and mindsets to connect and establish virtual relationships that are sometimes as tangible and influential as their in-person relationships.

That is why in recent years, and notably with the rise of the Islamic State (IS), there has been a sharp increase in research focused on the use of internet technologies by extremist organizations and terrorist groups to radicalize and recruit members (Hoffman, 2006; Inan, 2007; Payne, 2009; Pariser, 2011; Rieger et al., 2013; Von Behr et al., 2013; Conway, 2016; Gill et al., 2017; Reed et al., 2019; Howard et al., 2019, 2022; Kenyon et al., 2021, 2022; Binder and Kenyon, 2022; Hamid and Ariza, 2022). The decentralized nature of the internet, coupled with its global reach allows terrorists and extremists to disseminate their message, interact with sympathizers, and radicalize and recruit supporters with alarming impunity (Inan, 2007).

The online presence and activity of extremist and terrorist groups has risen sharply over the last fifteen years. "Exclusive or predominant online radicalization has [also] been on the rise" (Binder and Kenyon, 2022, p. 7). Research on the relationship between the internet and radicalization indicates that the internet provides more opportunities for a person to become radicalized, which, by extension, creates more opportunities for an individual to become self-radicalized without ever having any physical contact with a member of an extremist organization (von Behr et al., 2013). Also, what is probably most significant about online radicalization is that the internet has an accelerating influence on the radicalization process (von Behr et al., 2013), which helps explain the relatively swift radicalization of many supporters of the Islamic State (EUROPOL, 2016; Baele et al., 2020).

Among the few comparative studies of online versus offline radicalization and the related frequency and lethality of violence, the authors find that among those who have been radicalized solely online, due to their higher levels of isolation, the likelihood of information leakage and signaling is much lower for this group, which translates into more effective attacks, that are very difficult to detect and thwart, which means these attacks are more deadly (Hamm and Spaaij, 2017; Hamid and Ariza, 2022). Even among those studies of hybrid radicalization (online *and* offline), the authors recognize the exacerbating influence of the internet, and find that of the convicted extremists evaluated for their study, "67 percent on [the hybrid] radicalization pathway showed high levels of engagement, and 48 percent demonstrated high levels of intent" (Binder and Kenyon, 2022, p. 7; see Kenyon et al., 2021, p. 17).

The internet is significant to the radicalization process because of how extremist and terrorist groups are able to extend their influence and disseminate their ideological message beyond physical boundaries to connect with sympathizers and supporters worldwide. And as internet technologies become increasingly more innovative and evolve, if past behavior is a predictor, the likelihood is high that extremists and terrorists will quickly adapt in order to advance their objectives.

3.1.5 The Importance of Internet Videos to the Neural Process of Empathy

Studies on the relationship between visual emotional stimuli and brain activity have determined that complex naturalistic stimulus events (i.e. phenomenon depicted in movies and films) are related to complex neural events in the brain (Bartels and Zeki, 2004; Hasson et al., 2004; Jääskeläinen et al., 2008; Lankinen et al., 2014; Kauttonen et al., 2015).

This is because movies typically depict people in their natural settings and contexts; therefore, when exposed to a naturalistic visual stimulus, such as a video or video clip, subjects engage the action observation and imitation networks in the brain, a process referred to as "mirroring" which involves the activation of the mirror neuron system or MNS (Saxe et al., 2004; Peelen and Downing, 2005; Kanwisher and Yovel, 2006; Large et al., 2008; Jastorff and Orban, 2009; Abdollahi et al., 2013).

Understanding the process of mirroring in relation to visual emotional stimuli is important, especially in the context of viewing propaganda videos that portray extremist behavior and actions, mainly because the mirror-neuron system (MNS) comprises several networks that are activated not only when an individual observes the performance of a physical action by another (i.e. limbic and motor movements), but also when an individual observes the emotional expressions of another (i.e. empathetic processes and facial expressions) (Kilner and Lemon, 2013; Vanderwert and Nelson, 2014; Karimova et al., 2023).

At the most basic level, the MNS is responsible for the motor process of imitation, but at a more complex level, it is also responsible for an individual's ability to experience the cognitive processes of both empathy and persuasion, which are essential to stimulating the desire in an individual to imitate an observed behavior. However, while cognitive neuro-scientific studies have identified specific neural correlates that respond to persuasion, the neurocognitive networks associated with feeling persuaded involve the activation of several regions of the brain (DMPFC, pSTS, TP and left VLPFC) which are not simultaneous, and occur in response to different types of stimuli and stimulus events, which makes it difficult to isolate and observe the process of persuasion using EEG (Falk et al., 2010).

However, identifying and measuring cognitive empathy is a lot more straightforward. "Functions associated with social perception, empathy, and emotional

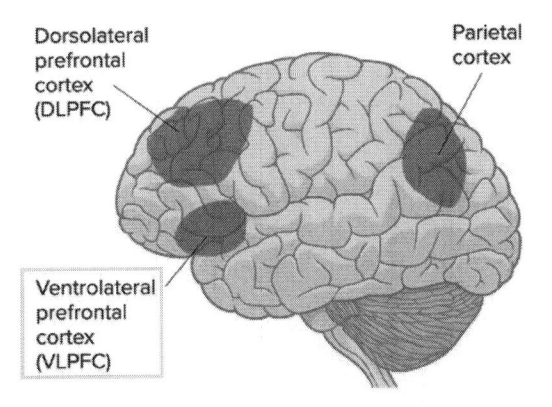

Figure 3 Ventrolateral prefrontal cortex (VLPFC) region of the brain

Source: Zanolie, K and E.A. Crone. 2018. *Stevens' Handbook of Experimental Psychology and Cognitive Neuroscience, 4th Ed.* John Wiley & Sons.

and cognitive assessment of social actions are known to be implemented by the MNS in humans," which can be observed in the ventromedial and ventrolateral prefrontal cortex regions of the brain (VMPFC and VLPFC) (Karimova et al., 2023, p. 1202). More importantly, a handful of studies have been able to effectively isolate and measure empathetic responses, which occur with MNS activity, and have determined that cognitive empathy can be observed specifically with the activation of the ventrolateral prefrontal cortex (VLPFC) region of the brain (Figure 3) when individuals are given tasks that require visual attention processing (like that of viewing a video clip) (Chory-Assad and Cicchirillo, 2005; Huppert et al., 2006; Singer et al., 2006; Himichi and Nomura, 2015; Majdandžić et al., 2016; Alkan et al., 2020; Karimova et al., 2023).

Consequently, given what we now know about neural observations of cognitive empathy, in this study we focus on brain activity in the VLPFC region in response to the stimulus events.

4 Data Acquisition and Experimental Procedures

4.1 Data Acquisition

4.1.1 Participants

This research was approved by the Institutional Research and Ethics Committee of the University of Nevada, Las Vegas.[11] The EEG data in this study were collected from eighty-six healthy adult-age subjects (47 males, 37 females, 2

---

[11] This project was reviewed and granted approval by the University of Nevada, Las Vegas Social/ Behavioral IRB as indicated in Federal regulatory statutes 45CFR46. Protocol ID: 1717170-2.

nonbinary) with an average age of 23.1 (SD = 4.8). All were self-reported U.S. citizens. Descriptive statistics and additional demographic details, as well as preliminary statistical models of the survey data are included in the Online Appendix (see Tables 14, 15, 16 and Document 1). Study participants were recruited using nonrandom captive sampling of university student and community volunteers in Washington D.C. and Las Vegas N.V. between January 2020 and September 2022.

4.1.2 The Interpersonal Reactivity Index Questionnaire

Baseline measures of empathy were first assessed using a validated English version (Baldner and McGinley, 2014) of the Interpersonal Reactivity Index (IRI) (Davis, 1980, 1983, 1996), a self-report questionnaire that evaluates four components of empathy: (1) perspective taking (the tendency to spontaneously adopt the psychological point of view of others); (2) fantasizing (the tendency to transpose ourselves imaginatively into fictional situations); (3) empathic concern (having feelings of sympathy or compassion toward others); and (4), personal distress (self-oriented feelings of personal anxiety or fear in response to seeing others in distress) (Chrysikou and Thompson, 2016). For each of the four empathetic measures there are seven questions for a total of twenty-eight questions; and the items are rated on a 5-point scale ranging from 1 (Does Not Describe Me Very Well) to 5 (Describes Me Very Well). The exception to this measurement rating includes the reverse scored items across the four empathetic components. These items are based upon an inverted scale.

Study participants were administered the IRI prior to the start of the experiment to determine their general capacity for empathy before stimulus exposure. It is important to note that the IRI was not developed to provide a measure of specific levels of empathy in the sense that its purpose is not to report on whether individuals demonstrate high or low levels of empathy, but rather, to "provide a measure of empathy-related constructs as they exist in normal [adult] populations."[12]

4.1.3 EEG Experiment

EEG data was collected using an Emotiv EPOC headset system. The headset consists of fourteen data-collecting electrodes and two reference electrodes, which were labeled and located in accordance with the international 10-20 EEG system. Figure 4 shows the 14 Emotiv EPOC headset electrode positions. For this study, we observed activity in the electrodes corresponding to the prefrontal cortex

---

[12] See Sara Hoffman. (2023). *Interpersonal Reactivity Index – Psychology | Eckerd College*. (2023, October 31). Psychology | Eckerd College. www.eckerd.edu/psychology/iri/.

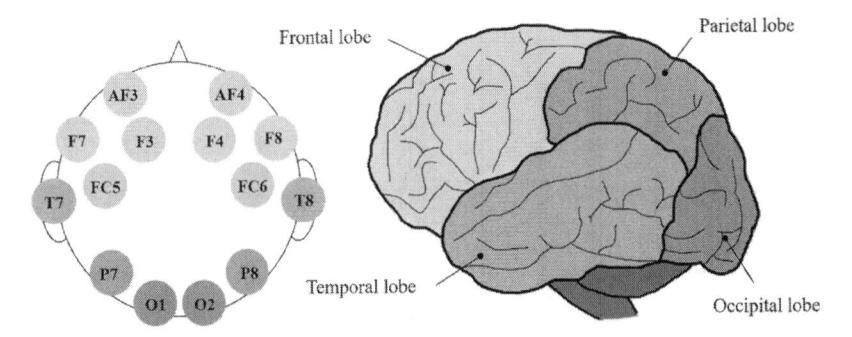

Figure 4 Emotiv EPOC headset electrode positioning

Source: Lee, Jiyoung, Tae Wan Kim, Lee Chan-Sik, and Choongwan Koo. (2022). "Integrated Approach to Evaluating the Effect of Indoor CO2 Concentration on Human Cognitive Performance and Neural Responses in Office Environment." *Journal of Management in Engineering* 38 (1). https://doi.org/10.1061/(asce)me.1943-5479.0000993.

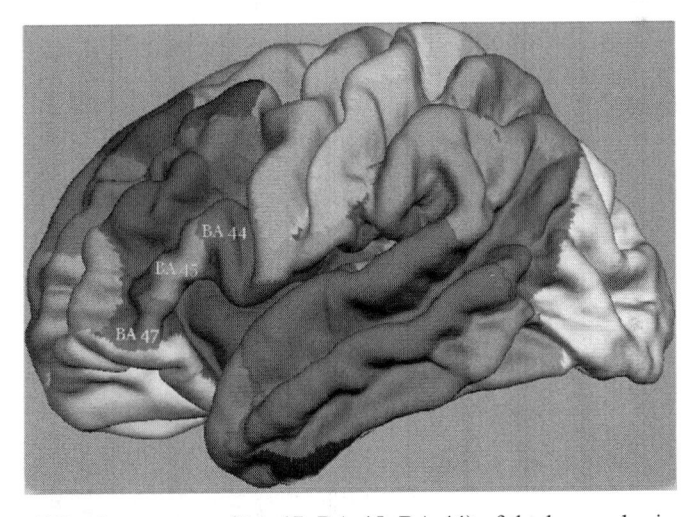

Figure 5 Brodmann areas (BA 47, BA 45, BA 44) of the human brain which correspond to the VLPFC

region of the brain, specifically the ventrolateral prefrontal cortex region (VLPFC) (i.e. nodes AF3, AF4, F7, F3, F4, F8). Figure 5 shows the specific VLPFC region of the brain where measurements were taken.

4.1.4 Data Collection Procedures

The aim of the experiment was to register neural activation (thus indicating an empathetic response) among the study participants using EEG. Neural activation (i.e. empathetic response) is captured using two measures. The first being an

$$E_A = \frac{E_\beta}{E_\alpha}$$

E_β= average beta power, E_α= average alpha power

Figure 6 Beta/alpha ratio-measure of empathetic arousal

individual's level of arousal during viewing. To determine the level of arousal (i.e. how excited the person is in response to the stimulus), we[13] calculated the beta/alpha ratio. To do this, we observed the nodal activity in four locations (i.e. electrodes) in the prefrontal cortex (i.e. AF3, AF4, F3, F4; Nodes AF3 and F3 allow us to focus specifically on neural activity in the VLPFC) which capture beta and alpha waves.

The use of the beta/alpha ratio is a standard measure of arousal using EEG (Figure 6) (Ramirez and Vamvakousis, 2012; Zheng and Lu, 2015; Kosiński et al., 2018). Beta waves are associated with alertness or an excited state of mind, while alpha waves are associated with a relaxed state or with brain inactivation. Therefore, alpha and beta wave information can be taken together as the beta/alpha ratio to give a reasonable index of the degree of arousal of a given person.

To calculate empathetic arousal (the beta/alpha ratio) we use the ratio band power values (Ramirez and Vamvakousis, 2012; Kosiński et al., 2018). "Band ratio measures, computed as the ratio of power between two frequency bands, are a common analysis measure in [neural and] electrophysiological recordings. Band ratio measures are typically interpreted as reflecting quantitative measures of periodic, or oscillatory activity" (Gasser et al., 1988; Saby and Marshall, 2012; Donoghue et al., 2020, p. 1). Accordingly, the higher the beta/alpha ratio band power value, the higher the state of arousal.

We determined that a beta/alpha ratio of 15 or below indicates low levels of arousal and is measured as "no arousal" suggesting that the participant is not responding to the visual stimulus. In contrast, a beta/alpha ratio of 16–34 indicates moderate levels of arousal, suggesting there is neural activation in response to the visual stimulus, but it is not significant. Finally, a beta/alpha ratio of 35 or above indicates high levels of arousal, suggesting there is neural activation in response to the visual stimulus that is significant (Ramirez and Vamvakousis, 2012; Zheng and Lu, 2015; Kosiński et al., 2018). In this study, only beta/alpha ratio scores of 35 or above are recorded as evidence of arousal in response to the stimuli.[14,15] These scores are then averaged as a single measure of arousal for those study subjects.

---

[13] Includes the author and four research assistants.

[14] Ratio band power is measured 1–50. Higher number, higher state of arousal.

[15] We used the Bonferroni test to confirm there is a statistically significant difference ($p<.05$) between the three levels of arousal.

The second measure of neural activation is captured by 2D viewing of delta brain wave activity in the prefrontal cortex region (i.e. nodes F7 and F8; Node F7 allows us to focus specifically on neural activity in the VLPFC) and is used to indicate the presence of cognitive empathy. Studies have shown that delta brain activity during an awakened state corresponds to cognitive empathetic processing (Yan et al., 2008; Neumann and Westbury, 2011; Neumann et al., 2015). Thus, delta wave activation indicates the presence of cognitive-empathy during an awakened state[16] when there is prefrontal activity, specifically that of left frontal activity or dominance[17] (Himichi and Nomura, 2015). Figure 7 provides an example of delta activity in response to the experimental stimulus.

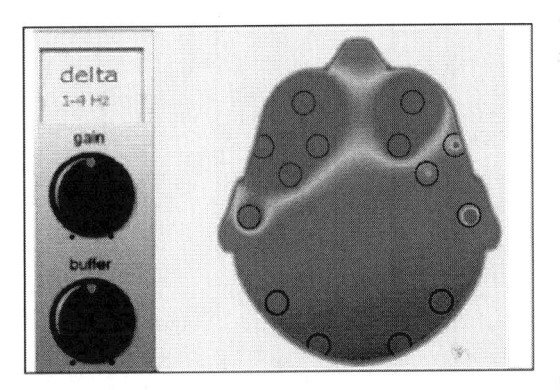

Figure 7 Study Participant A – delta activity during stimulus video 1 (i.e. Segment 4 – ISIS Soldier: 3m27s to 3m39s).

Note: Delta wave activation corresponds to the presence of cognitive-empathy during an awakened state when there is left-frontal activity or left frontal dominance as we see here.

---

[16] Due to its low frequency during awakened states, delta waves are best captured using brain visualization software than with raw EEG data, which would overestimate beta and alpha waves in order to accurately measure Delta waves. The buffer would have to be set very low to make it more sensitive and would inaccurately measure beta and alpha waves. Thus, it would introduce a lot of noise, which is why we don't use the EEG raw data for delta measures and it is also why we could not simultaneously use the brain visualization activity of alpha and beta waves alone without the corresponding raw EEG data measures. However, to record the raw EEG data of delta activity, we observed nodal activity in the F7 and F8 electrodes.

[17] Right frontal activation is important, but it is not essential for the measure of empathy. Therefore, if empathy is present, 2D imaging will reveal either left frontal activity, or left front activity in addition to right frontal activity.

4.1.5 Outcome Measure
$E_A + \Delta =$ Empathetic Response

E_A = Arousal in the prefrontal cortex (i.e. nodes AF3, AF4, F3, F4) as measured by Beta/Alpha Ratio (E_A)

$+$

Δ = Delta brain wave activity (i.e. prefrontal cortex activity, especially left frontal activity or dominance; nodes F7 and F8) as measured by 2D brainwave visualization

4.2 Experimental Procedure, Inclusion Criteria, and Audiovisual Stimuli

The experiment was organized into two studies. In Study One, radical Islamic propaganda videos are used as the stimuli to observe participants' neural activity for the presence of empathetic arousal in response to the videos' messaging. Whereas, in Study Two, right-wing extremist propaganda videos are used as the stimuli in order to observe the presence of empathetic arousal in response to the messaging presented in the selected videos.

Subjects were asked to view a total of six videos – three radical Islamic videos (for Study One) and three right-wing extremist videos (for Study Two). Each of the three videos for Study One, and then for Study Two, depicts a specific type of propaganda messaging device used by extremists and/or terrorists in online videos. These include (1) Narrative; (2) Victim Portrayals, and (3) Charismatic Authority/Leader.

The inclusion criteria for the stimulus videos were as follows:

1. Videos could be no shorter than one minute and no longer than fifteen minutes.[18]
2. The date of creation and dissemination of the video could not take place before 2012 (time period was 2012–2022).
3. All videos had to either feature a currently operating terrorist or extremist organization, or promote a contemporary extremist ideology that is tied to an active extremist organization.

---

[18] While there does not appear to be any consensus regarding video length with regard to neural activation and processing, studies on subject engagement of audiovisual material, specifically within the context of education, suggest that videos six minutes in length promote optimal retention and engagement, and that retention and engagement diminish significantly after fifteen minutes. See Guo et al., 2014; Berg et al., 2014; Brame, 2016; Alexander and Poch, 2017; Carmichael et al., 2018; Gonzalez, 2020.

4. For the videos featuring a charismatic leader, the subject had to still be living at the time of the experiment.[19]
5. The videos had to be directed toward a Western audience as demonstrated by the production of the videos in English or that they feature English subtitles.
6. The videos had to be easily accessible using the internet, and ideally hosted on YouTube.[20]
7. The videos had to feature one of the three types of propaganda messaging devices: the Narrative, Victim Portrayals, or the Charismatic Authority/Leader.
8. The videos had to be anonymously produced, clearly produced by the terrorist or extremist organization, sanctioned by the terrorist or extremist organization, or explicitly promote a contemporary extremist ideology.
9. The videos had to promote an extremist ideology that is espoused by at least one active transnational terrorist or extremist organization.
10. For the videos that represent victim portrayals, they had to feature Muslim or Arab victims (in the case of radical Islamic terrorism/extremism), and White, Christian, heterosexual presenting victims (in the case of right-wing extremism).
11. For the videos that represent victim portrayals, the subjects could be physical victims of violence, or symbolic victims (i.e. culture wars)

Using these inclusion criteria, twenty-six radical Islamic extremist videos were identified, and thirty-seven right-wing extremist videos were identified. They were then divided by messaging type, and one video from each messaging type was randomly selected, for a total of six videos (i.e. three radical Islamic videos and three right-wing extremist videos). Of the sample of six videos, the longest was eleven minutes and thirty-five seconds and the shortest was one-minute and forty seconds.

Prior to stimulus exposure, a one-minute baseline was established by showing the study participants a blank screen. The stimulus videos were shown to each participant in random order, with a 30-second blank screen baseline in between each showing.

For each stimulus video, corresponding periods of arousal (as measured by EEG beta/alpha ratio) and cognitive empathy (as measured by 2D visual delta activity) are recorded and numbered by segments. At the conclusion of the entire experiment, the segments that were salient across the majority of study

---

[19] There is speculation regarding whether the subject died in 2019. However, the subject was verified to still be living at the time of the initial data collection. Mainly, we did not want to include videos of a defunct group and/or obsolete leader.

[20] The reason for this is because we did not want a video that could only be viewed on the dark web, which cannot be readily accessed by an average person with basic internet literacy and technological skills.

participants ($n > 43$) were identified. These segments were labeled empathetic arousing. Each segment was then reviewed to identify the imagery, linguistic elements, and rhetorical patterns capable of arousing an empathetic response. Coding was conducted by the author, three undergraduate interns, and one graduate student research assistant. Inter-rater reliability checks were conducted to ensure consistency.

4.2.1 Study One: Radical Islamic Extremism and Terrorism Video Stimuli

1. **Stimulus 1A – Narrative**
   No Respite (2015; 4m14s) – A traditional ISIS propaganda video featuring strong narrative elements that are presented in English.[21]
2. **Stimulus 2A – Victim Portrayal**
   Anonymous video clip honoring the victims of the Christchurch Terrorist Attack (2019; 1m40s) – A silent video clip with English subtitles featuring strong imagery and elements of Muslim victims at the hands of far-right extremist violence.[22]
3. **Stimulus 3A – Charismatic Leader/Authority**
   Al-Shabaab: Exclusive interview with Sheikh Ali Dhere (2013; 4m06s) – A traditional media interview with Al-Shabaab leader and official spokes-person that includes English subtitles and features a "charismatic leader" and strong narrative elements.[23]

4.2.2 Study Two: Right-Wing/Alt-Right Extremism and Terrorism Video Stimuli

1. **Stimulus 1B – Narrative**
   You Can't Be Racist to White People (2019; 11m35s) – A short video by right-wing extremist influencer The White Rose on discrimination against whites by U.S. universities.[24]
2. **Stimulus 2B – Victim Portrayal**
   A Rash of Attacks against White People–None Are Being Charged as Hate Crimes (2020; 12m56s) – A news video presented on the *DailyWire*, which is a self-described conservative news source website that publishes counterculture and alt-right content. The video features strong victim portrayal propaganda elements that advance the argument that when non-white perpetrators commit

---

[21] *No Respite*. ISIS. Filmed/Uploaded, December 17, 2015. Video Length: 04m:14s. https://nypost.com/2015/12/17/help-im-in-an-isis-propaganda-video/.
[22] *Christchurch Terrorist Attack.* Unknown/No Group Affiliation. Filmed/Uploaded, March 17, 2019. Video Length: 01m:40s. www.youtube.com/watch?v=cHR8h_g3Mj4.
[23] *Al-Shabaab: Exclusive interview with Sheikh Ali Dhere.* Al-Shabaab. Filmed/Uploaded, December 16, 2013. Video Length: 04m:06s. www.youtube.com/watch?v=TIhHxlm_WZE.
[24] *You Can't Be Racist to White People.* White Rose/No Group Affiliation. Filmed/Uploaded, February 27th, 2019. Video Length: 11m:35s. www.bitchute.com/video/7bGSYVxyCWhy/.

crimes against white Americans, they are not classified as hate crimes by the justice system in the United States.[25]

3. **Stimulus 3B – Charismatic Leader/Authority**
   Rebranding White Nationalism: Inside Richard Spencer's Alt-Right (2016; 11m8s) – An expose by *The Atlantic* on white supremacist and alt-right leader Richard Spencer. The video includes a combination of an interview with Spencer, along with clips from one of Spencer's speeches where he calls for supporters to advance the agenda of the white nationalist movement.[26]

5 Analyses and Findings

5.1 The Interpersonal Reactivity Index Questionnaire

The Interpersonal Reactivity Index (IRI) was administered to all research participants pre-experiment to determine the subjects' capacity for empathy (see Online Appendix Document 2 for questionnaire). For each of the four empathetic components (i.e. Perspective Taking, Fantasy, Empathetic Concern, and Personal Distress), there are seven questions for a total of twenty-eight questions; and the items are rated on a 5-point scale ranging from 1 (Does Not Describe Me Very Well) to 5 (Describes Me Very Well). Therefore, the cumulative measure for each empathetic component ranges from seven to thirty-five, with seven corresponding to the "lowest level"[27] of empathy and thirty-five corresponding to the "highest level"[28] of empathy. The exception to this measurement rating is the reverse scored items across the four measures of empathy. These items are based upon an inverted scale. Therefore, prior to calculating the scores, the responses for the items on the inverted scale were recoded to be consistent with the standard measurement scale. Each participant then received an aggregate score for each empathetic component; the average of those scores was then calculated, along with the standard deviation. Those results are presented in Table 5.

Across the four empathetic measures, the study participants demonstrated comparable capacities for empathy to subjects observed in psychological studies that also utilize the IRI in research on empathy and some aspect of

---

[25] *A Rash of Attacks against White People–None Are Being Charged as Hate Crimes.* Daily Wire/ No Group Affiliation. Filmed/Uploaded. June 22, 2020. Video Length: 12m:56s. www.youtube .com/watch?v=b806JHG9eKI.

[26] *Rebranding White Nationalism: Inside Richard Spencer's Alt-Right.* The Atlantic/No Group Affiliation. Filmed/Uploaded, December 15, 2016. Video Length: 11m:8s. www.youtube.com/ watch?v=kVeZ0_Lhazw.

[27] As noted in Section 3, the IRI was not developed to provide a measure of specific levels of empathy in the sense that its purpose is not to report on whether individuals demonstrate high or low levels of empathy, but rather, to "provide a measure of empathy-related constructs as they exist in normal [adult] populations." See, Sara Hoffman. (2023). *Interpersonal Reactivity Index – Psychology | Eckerd College.* (2023, October 31). Psychology | Eckerd College. www.eckerd.edu/psychology/ iri/.

[28] Ibid.

Table 5 Interpersonal Reactivity Index (IRI) findings[a]

Empathy Trait	Mean	Standard Deviation
1. IRI-PT (Perspective Taking)	29.4	5.21
2. IRI-FS (Fantasy Scale)	30.2	4.31
3. IRI-EC (Empathetic Concern)	32.7	4.21
4. IRI-PD (Personal Distress)	22.9	3.63

[a] See Appendix, Table 17 for Cronbach's Alpha for the IRI Sub-Scales.

nonnormative attitudes (i.e. risk for intergroup conflict, aggression, interethnic tension, risk for violent extremism) (Table 5) (Feddes et al., 2015; Influs et al., 2019; Tabares and Durán Palacio, 2021).[29,30]

5.2 Establishing a Baseline and Reference Measure

Upon establishing the study participants' empathetic capacities, the next step was to determine a baseline measure for each participant. Figure 8 reflects the baseline of an average study participant where there is no indication of arousal or empathy. The calculated beta/alpha ratio is less than or equal to 15, and there is no significant delta wave brain activity. During periods of nonexposure to stimulus events, participants were shown a blank screen to return them to baseline before moving on to the next stimulus event.

Figure 9 provides a reference measure from an average study participant where there is an indication of moderate arousal, but no indication of empathy. The calculated beta/alpha ratio is between 16 and 34 indicating moderate levels of arousal, but there is no significant delta wave brain activity. The reference measure is used as a comparison tool to distinguish between stimulus events that generate an empathetic response and produce empathetic arousal, from those

---

[29] There are additional studies which also use the IRI in their research on violent radical political behavior, but the authors do not present their study participant mean scores on the IRI, so we are unable to observe any commonalities between our research and those studies. See Emile G. Bruneau, Mina Cikara and Rebecca Saxe, "Parochial Empathy Predicts Reduced Altruism and the Endorsement of Passive Harm," *Social Psychological and Personality Science* 8, no. 8 (2017): 934–942; Cohen, "The Effects of Empathy on Intergroup Conflict and Aggression"; Arlinda Rrustemi, "Measuring the Impact of the Lifestory Approach on Preventing and Countering Violent Extremism," *Hague Centre for Strategic Studies* (2020), www.jstor.org/stable/resrep24838 (accessed October 15, 2021); Sara Savage and Patricia Fearon, "Increasing Cognitive Complexity and Meta-Awareness among At-Risk Youth in Bosnia-Herzegovina in Order to Reduce Risk of Extremism and Interethnic Tension," *Peace and Conflict: Journal of Peace Psychology* 27, no. 2 (2021): 225–239.

[30] For general interest studies that do allow for IRI data comparisons, See Davis, "Measuring Individual Differences in Empathy"; Kim De Corte, Ann Buysse, Lesley L. Verhofstadt, et al., "Measuring Empathic Tendencies: Reliability and Validity of the Dutch Version of the Interpersonal Reactivity Index," *Psychologica Belgica* 47, no. 4 (2007): 235–260.

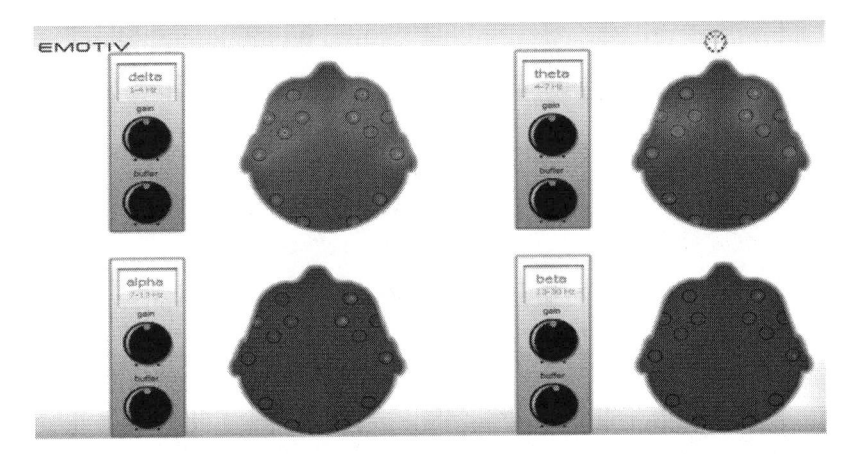

Figure 8 Baseline (i.e. no arousal and no empathy)

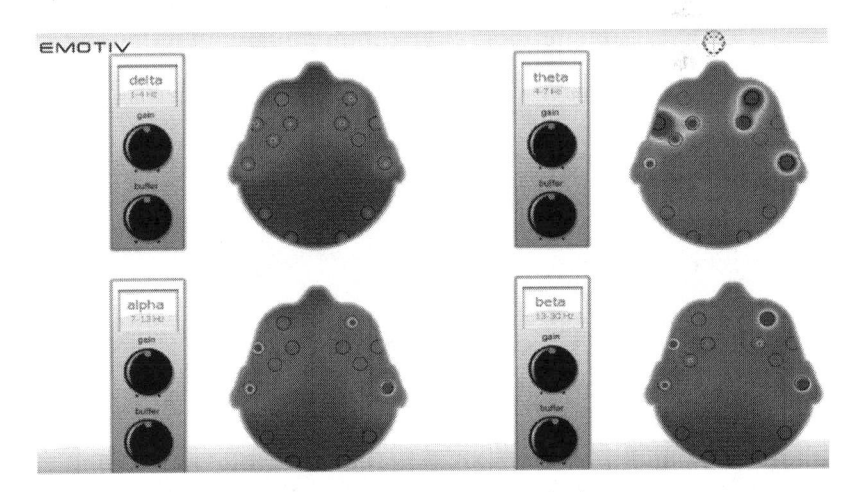

Figure 9 Arousal but no empathy

Note: $16 \leq E_A \leq 34$

stimulus events that do not generate an empathetic response or result in a state of arousal indicative of high levels of empathy.

5.3 Content Analysis and EEG Experiment

5.3.1 Study One: Radical Islamic Terrorism and Extremism

Narrative

In Table 6 we report the content analytic findings[31] for the Narrative stimulus video, *No Respite*, which employs the use of the narrative as its propaganda

---

[31] Unredacted materials found in Section 5.3 are available from the author.

Table 6 Stimulus 1A: ISIS: No Respite (Narrative)

Segment Label	Time Start	Time End	Content Elements	# of Study Participants	Average E_A
1. U.S. Presidents	0:47	0:52	Words: Fornicators, Liars; Image: U.S. Presidents Obama, Bush, Clinton; Theme: U.S. Flag, U.S. Capitol, American Patriotism; Imagery: Dark colors, unflattering pictures of U.S. presidents	56	38
2. United by Islam	1:30	1:37	Words: No difference between Arab or non-Arab, Black or White Man; Image: Multiracial/Ethnic Soldiers together; Theme: Racial equality, united by Islam; Imagery: Bright colors, unity	61	40
3. U.S. Soldiers*	2:03	2:29	Words: Dead, Suicidal, 18 U.S. soldiers commit suicide per day; Image: U.S. Soldiers, depression, pills; Theme: Defeated America; Imagery: Dark colors, overcast	64	42
4. ISIS Soldier	3:27	3:39	Words: Bring it on; Image: ISIS soldier waving ISIS flag; Theme: Strength, pride, challenge to the West; Imagery: Orange colors, fire, caliphate in background, expansive	60	37
5. No Respite	3:50	4:08	Words: So resolve upon your plan and call upon your associates . . . .They carry it out upon me and do not give me respite; Theme: A verse from the Qur'an that is provocative and challenging the West; Imagery: Words juxtaposed over a bright image of the Earth.	61	38

Figure 10 Stimulus video 1A – Segment 2: United by Islam (1m30s to 1m37s)

device. In the 4min 14s video we identified five segments where there was significant arousal across a majority ($n > 43$) of study participants and significant delta wave brain activity indicating the presence of empathy. The highest Average E_A (i.e. arousal as measured by the beta/alpha ratio) is recorded for the segment titled *U.S. Soldiers* (Average $E_A = 42$), which features images of dejected U.S. soldiers and discusses the rates of suicide and PTSD among U.S. soldiers returning from war. While the lowest Average E_A score is recorded for the segment titled *ISIS Soldiers* (Average $E_A = 37$), which features the image of an ISIS soldier waving the ISIS flag, and the narrator is using language that challenges the strength and fortitude of the West. Another segment that reports a strong measure of arousal (Average $E_A = 40$) is that of the segment titled *United by Islam* (Figure 10). This segment promotes equality among the men who become ISIS soldiers and displays strong elements of loyalty and camaraderie.

With respect to the 2D brain visualization findings, Figure 11 provides an example of significant delta wave activity for four randomly selected study participants while viewing Segment 2 (*United by Islam*) of the stimulus video. The red area in the image indicates there is significant delta wave activity in the VLPFC region of the brain during the highlighted segment. Consequently, the findings suggest that the presence of high levels of arousal combined with significant delta wave activity indicate an empathetic response to the denoted segments.

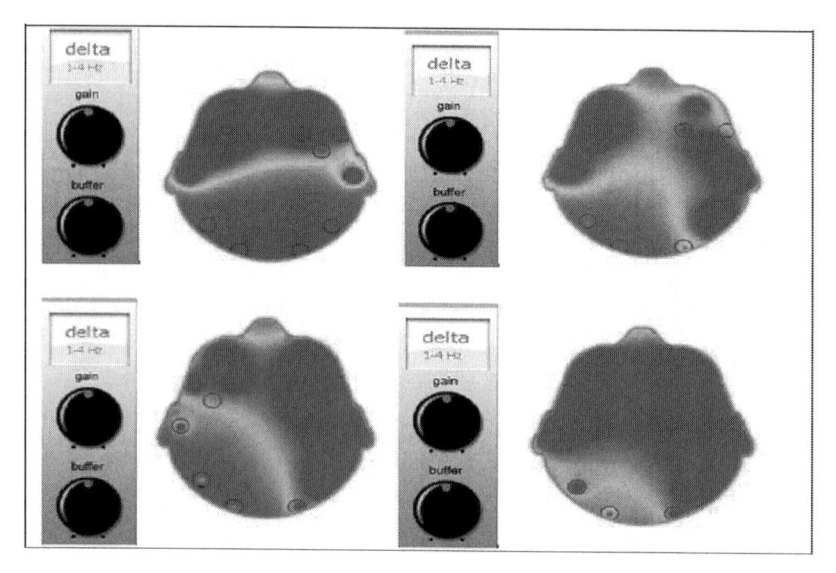

Figure 11 Sample of four randomly selected study participants and the delta activity imaging results for stimulus video 1A – Segment 2: United by Islam (1m30s to 1m37s)

Victim Portrayal

In Table 7 we report the findings of the content analysis for the Victim Portrayal stimulus video, which is a tribute to the victims of the Christchurch terrorist attack. This video employs the use of victim portrayals as its propaganda device. In the 1min 40s video we identified seven segments where there was significant arousal across a majority of the study subjects along with significant delta activity. The highest Average E_A is recorded for the segments titled *Brave Wife* (Average E_A = 49), *Youngest Victim* (Average E_A = 49) (Figure 12), and *Young Father* (Average E_A = 48). The common themes that unify these three segments are that they either feature a caretaker or a child, and they highlight familial connections. The lowest Average E_A score is recorded for the segment titled *Attack Scenes* (Average E_A = 45), which features images of the violence and destruction indicative of the scene of a terrorist or extremist attack, but does not feature a specific person, so there is likely less emotional attachment to the segment than with the other segments.

With respect to the 2D brain visualization findings, Figure 13 provides an example of significant delta wave activity for four randomly selected study participants while viewing segment ten (*Youngest Victim*) of the stimulus video. The

Table 7 Stimulus 2A: Christchurch terrorist attack (victim portrayal)

Segment Label	Time Start	Time End	Elements	# of Study Participants	Average E_A
6. Attack Scenes	0:01	0:14	Words: Death toll at 50, 11 still hospitalized; Imagery: Man on stretcher, flower memorial; Theme: victim toll, somber; Imagery: neutral colors, paying tribute	62	42
7. Seventy-One-Year-Old Worshiper	0:20	0:30	Words: Died trying to save other worshippers; Came from Afghanistan to escape the Soviet invasion; Theme: victim, somber, serious; Imagery: Black and white mage of an elderly man with a young child that is replaced with a picture of the victim as a younger man.	78	45
8. Male Teenage Victim	0:42	0:48	Words: Teenager, dreamed of being a footballer; Image: smiling male teen; Theme: victim, somber; Imagery: black and white colors to highlight impact	82	47
9. Young Father	0:51	0:57	Words: New father, played for his local football team; Image: smiling father holding his child; Theme: somber; Imagery: black and white colors to highlight impact	82	48
10. Syrian Refugee	1:00	1:11	Words: Survived civil war in Syria, came to New Zealand to find safe haven, one of his sons was also a victim; Image: smiling middle aged man; Theme: victim, somber; Imagery: black and white colors to highlight impact	80	46
11. Brave Wife	1:12	1:23	Words: Wife died trying to protect husband who was ill and confined to a wheelchair; Image: smiling portrait of young Muslim woman; Theme: somber; Imagery: bright colors of woman's yellow hijab against black and white background to highlight impact and distinguish female victim	83	49
12. Youngest Victim	1:26	1:35	Words: Youngest victim was three years old; Image: little boy; Theme: victim, somber; Imagery: black and white colors to highlight impact	84	49

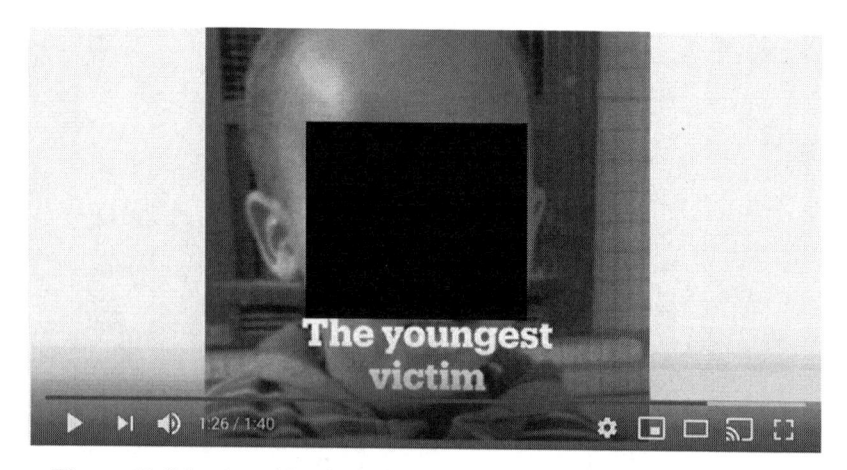

Figure 12 Stimulus video 2A – Segment 10: Youngest Victim (1m26s to 1m35s)

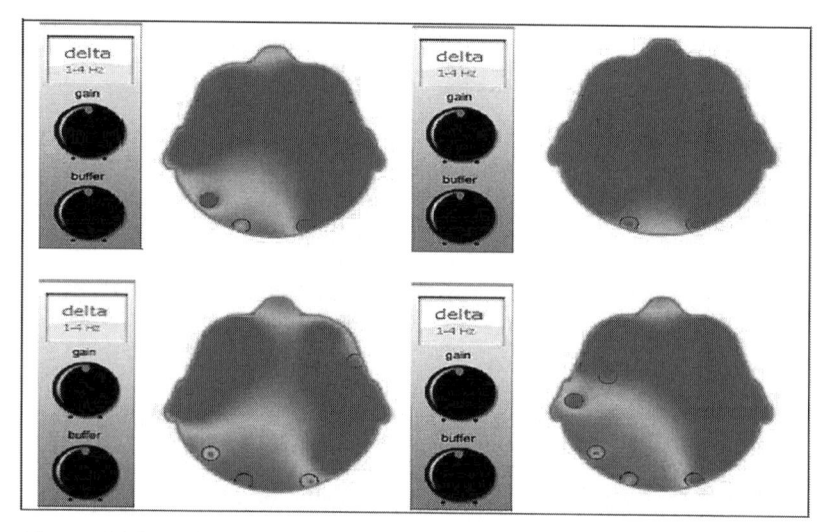

Figure 13 Sample of four randomly selected study participants and the delta activity imaging results for stimulus video 2A – Segment 10: The Youngest Victim (1m26s to 1m35s)

combined presence of high levels of arousal with significant delta wave activity indicates the presence of an empathetic response during the denoted segments.

Charismatic Leader/Authority

In Table 8 we report the findings of the content analysis for the Charismatic Authority/Leader stimulus video, which features an interview with the

Table 8 Stimulus 3A: Interview with Sheikh Ali Dhere (Charismatic Authority/Leader)

Segment Label	Time Start	Time End	Elements	# of Study Participants	Average E_A
11. Foreigners Leave	0:10	1:00	Words: Free our country, govern our people under Islamic law, foreigners aren't interested in helping Somalia, they didn't help during the clan wars, they need to leave, it's better for Somalis; Image: Sheikh Dhere in keffiyeh and combat fatigues (BDUs); Theme/Imagery: Outside, greenery, nature, rugged	57	37
12. Westgate Mall Attack in Kenya*	1:35	2:23	Words: We told them to leave our country, but they ignored us, so we had to send a message, it happened at the heart of their country, they are weak; Image: Sheikh Dhere in keffiyeh and combat fatigues (BDUs); Theme/Imagery: Outside, greenery, nature, rugged, provoking, challenging display of strength.	58	38
13. No Colonizers	2:40	2:50	Words: We are not going to work with colonizers, we would never bow down to colonizers; Image: Sheikh Dhere in keffiyeh and combat fatigues (BDUs) holding assault rifle casually over his lap; Theme/Imagery: Outside, greenery, nature, rugged, invokes toughness	56	37
14. British Problem	3:10	3:35	Words: The British are colonizers, they are supporting the Kenyan mercenaries, second to America, they are the biggest problem, invitation to British and American Muslims to join; Image: Sheikh Dhere in keffiyeh and combat fatigues (BDUs) holding assault rifle casually over his lap; Theme/Imagery: Outside, greenery, nature, rugged, invokes toughness	56	36

Al-Shabaab spokesperson, Sheikh Ali Dhere. This video features the use of the Charismatic Authority/Leader as its propaganda device. In the 4min 6s video we identified four segments where there was significant arousal and significant delta activity among the majority of study participants. The highest Average E_A recorded for the segment titled *Westgate Mall Attack in Kenya* (Average E_A = 38), which shows Sheikh Dhere speaking bluntly and defiantly about the terrorist attack in Kenya. Two other segments which indicate strong measures of arousal are that of *Foreigners Leave* (Average E_A = 37) and *No Colonizers* (Average E_A = 37). The commonalities between these two segments are that Sheikh Dhere speaks of the independence of the Somali state, and that the interference of the West is harmful to Somalia and unwelcome. The lowest Average E_A score is recorded for the segment titled *British Problem* (Average E_A = 36), which is where Sheikh Dhere identifies the British as the problem, although he notes they are second to America, and he invites British and American sympathizers of Al Shabaab to join them (Figure 14).

Figure 15 provides an example of significant delta wave activity for four randomly selected study participants while viewing Segment 13 (*British Problem*) of the stimulus video. The combined presence of high levels of arousal with significant delta wave activity indicates an empathetic response during the denoted segments.

Figure 14 Stimulus video 3A – Segment 13: British Problem (3m10s to 3m35s)

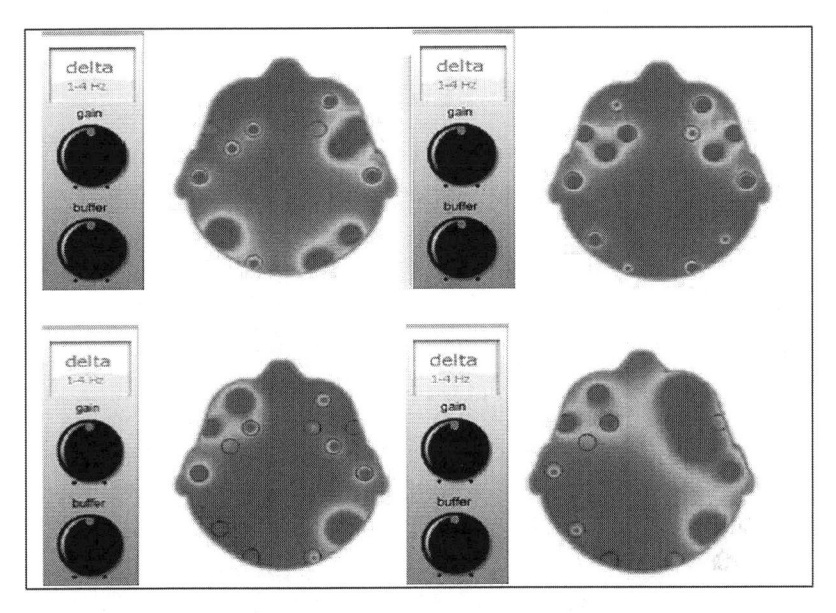

Figure 15 Sample of four randomly selected study participants and the delta activity imaging results for stimulus video 3A – Segment 13: British Problem (3m10s to 3m35s)

5.3.2 Study Two: Right-Wing and Alt-Right Terrorism and Extremism

Narrative

In Table 9 we report the content analytic findings for the right-wing/alt-right extremist Narrative stimulus video, *You Can't Be Racist to White People,* which employs the use of the narrative as its propaganda device. In the 11min 35s video we identified seven segments where there is significant arousal across a majority of study participants ($n > 43$), and significant delta activity, indicating the presence of empathy. The highest Average E_A (i.e. arousal as measured by beta/alpha ratio) is recorded for the segment titled *Racism Is Not about Power . . .* (Average $E_A = 42$), which features images of right-wing influencer The White Rose discussing several definitions of racism. While the lowest Average E_A score is recorded for the segment titled *Racism against Whites Is a Serious Problem* (Average $E_A = 36$), which once again features the image of The White Rose talking about the privileges of western society, alongside a montage of clips featuring controversial practices that take place in non-Western nations. Another segment that reports a strong measure of arousal (Average $E_A = 40$) is that of the segment titled *Black People Are Targeted by the Police Because They Are Criminals* (Figure 16). This segment features The White Rose alongside a montage of figures and quotes that support her assertion

Table 9 Stimulus 1B: You Can't Be Racist to White People (narrative)

Segment Label	Time Start	Time End	Elements	# of Study Participants	Average E_A
1. Racism Is Not About Power	0:22	0:48	Words: Racism has nothing to do with power but is defined as feelings of racial superiority; Image: Right-wing extremist influencer, the White Rose in a rose-colored shirt, wearing makeup and rose-colored lipstick, against a black background; Theme/Imagery: Inflammatory, brash, blunt, close focus on speaker's face for emphasis and impact	57	42
2. Derogatory References to Black People and Mentally Disabled People	0:53	1:06	Words: Are they children; are they mentally retarded; Image: Right-wing extremist influencer, the White Rose in a rose-colored shirt, wearing makeup and rose-colored lipstick, against a black background; Theme/Imagery: Inflammatory, brash, blunt, close focus on speaker's face for emphasis and impact	50	38
3. Black People are Racist	1:38	3:58	Words: White lives don't matter, White people are devils, I don't like them, I don't trust them; Image: Montage of clips of Black people making statements about White people; Theme/Imagery: Inflammatory, sensational, shocking, aggressive. Clips portray the (black) speakers as angry, passionate.	54	38
4. Racism is a Conspiracy Theory	4:39	5:00	Words: Institutionalized racism in the U.S. is a conspiracy theory, The President (Obama) is black; Image: the White Rose and a montage of clips of black celebrities and Obama; Theme/Imagery: Inflammatory, brash, blunt, close focus on speaker's face for emphasis and impact, clips of high profile African Americans emphasize that black people are not oppressed.	51	37

5. Black People are Targeted by the Police Because They Are Criminals	5:13	6:11	Words: All minorities are not targeted by the police, black people are, refers to black people as thugs; Image: The White Rose and a montage of tables that cite statistics on black homicides; Theme/Imagery: Inflammatory, brash, blunt, close focus on speaker's face for emphasis and impact, figures support the speaker's argument regarding the criminality of black people and that the police shootings are justified to save lives	54	40
6. The West is the Best	9:23	10:00	Words: If you are living in a western country you do not get to say f*ck white people, while benefiting from western privileges; Image: the White Rose and a montage of clips depicting controversial practices in non-western countries; Theme/ Imagery: Inflammatory, brash, blunt, close focus on speaker's face for emphasis and impact, clips of extreme practices to support argument of western superiority.	48	37
7. Racism Against Whites is A Serious Problem	10:54	11:25	Words: Racism against whites is a serious problem … I don't see us overcoming racism when people are allowed to be horrible to white people; Image: The White Rose in a rose-colored shirt, wearing makeup and rose-colored lipstick, against a black background; Theme/Imagery: Inflammatory, brash, blunt, close focus on speaker's face for emphasis and impact, speaking directly to the camera/audience.	47	36

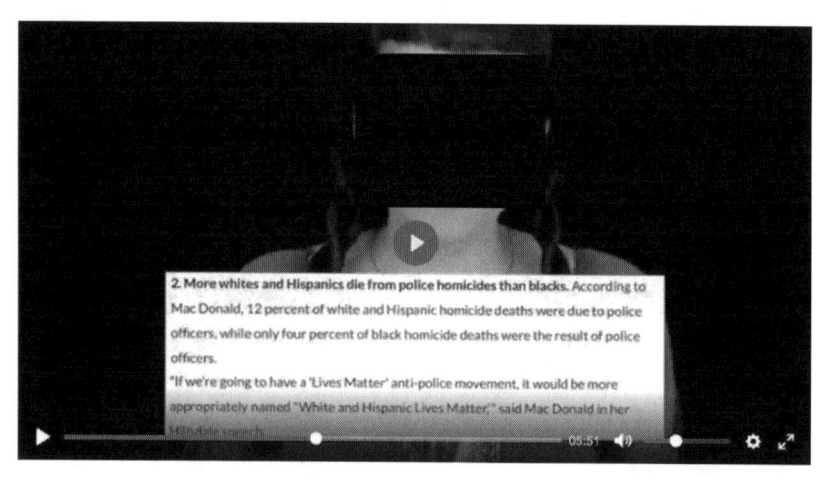

Figure 16 Stimulus video 1B – Segment 5: Black People Are Targeted by the
Police Because They Are Criminals (5m13s to 6m11s)

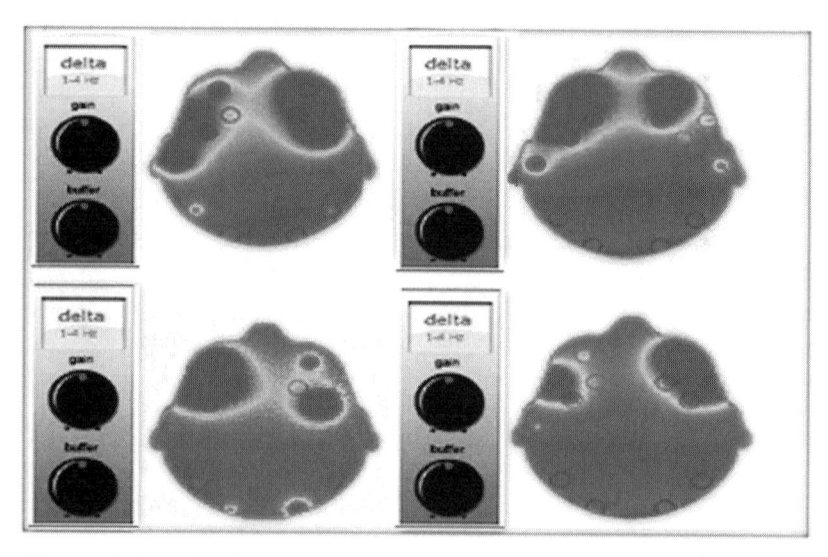

Figure 17 Sample of four randomly selected study participants and the delta
activity imaging results for stimulus video 1B – Segment 5: Black People Are
Targeted by the Police Because They Are Criminals (5m13s to 6m11s)

that targeted police violence in Black communities is warranted because they
are "thugs" and "criminals."

With respect to the 2D brain visualization findings, Figure 17 provides an
example of significant delta wave activity for a sample of four randomly

selected study participants while viewing Segment 5 (*Black People Are Targeted* ...) of the stimulus video. The red area in the image indicates there is significant delta wave activity in the VLPFC region of the brain during the highlighted segment. Consequently, the findings suggest the combined presence of high levels of arousal with significant delta wave activity indicate an empathetic response to the denoted segments.

Victim Portrayal

In Table 10 we report the findings of the right-wing/alt-right extremism content analysis for the Victim Portrayal stimulus video, which is a news video from the alt-right website, the *DailyWire*. The video features strong victim portrayal propaganda elements which advance the argument that when non-white perpetrators commit crimes against white Americans, they are not charged with a hate crime because of the assumption that non-whites can't be racist or commit racial violence toward whites.

This video employs the use of victim portrayals as its propaganda device. In the 12min 56s video we identified five segments where there is significant arousal across a majority of the study subjects along with significant delta brain activity. The highest Average E_A is recorded for the segment titled *Attacks on White Senior Citizens* (Average E_A = 49), which features right-wing podcaster, Matt Walsh, talking about cases where white senior citizens have been attacked by African Americans and how these incidents have not received comparable news coverage or similar feelings of outrage if the races of the victim and perpetrator had been reversed. The lowest Average E_A score is recorded for the segment titled *Not a Proponent of Hate Crimes* (Average E_A = 43), which features Matt Walsh discussing how he doesn't believe crimes should be labeled as hate crimes. Another segment that reports a strong measure of arousal (Average E_A = 48) is that of the segment titled *Black Male Attack on White Male* (Figure 18). This segment features the image of a Black male standing over and verbally threatening a white male on the floor of a department store.

With respect to the 2D brain visualization findings, Figure 19 provides an example of significant delta wave activity for a sample of four randomly selected study participants while viewing Segment 8 (*Black Male Attack on White Male*) of the stimulus video. The combined presence of high levels of arousal with significant delta wave activity indicates the presence of an empathetic response during the denoted segments.

Table 10 Stimulus 2B: A Rash of Attacks against White People – None Are Being Charged as Hate Crimes (victim portrayal)

Segment Label	Time Start	Time End	Elements	# of Study Participants	Average E_A
8. Black Male Attack on White Male	0:23	0:43	Words: Black man attack on white male Macy's employee; Image: Of a black man standing over and verbally threatening a white man on the ground; Theme: serious, inflammatory; Imagery: neutral colors, close frame for emphasis	80	48
9. No Charges Filed	2:12	3:12	Words: No hate crime charges filed; Image: Podcaster Matt Walsh is sitting in front of a bookshelf and brick wall; Theme: serious, victim, shock factor; Image: Warm, earthy, rustic colors to foster message connection and relatability	75	44
10. Attacks on White Senior Citizens	4:19	5:00	Words: 92-year-old woman brutally attacked, 76-year- old white man violently attacked; Image: Podcaster Matt Walsh is sitting in front of a bookshelf and brick wall; Theme: inflammatory, sensational, victim language; Image: Warm, earthy, rustic colors to foster message connection and relatability	84	49
11. Not a Proponent of Hate Crimes	9:07	9:44	Words: Do not believe violent crimes should be labeled along a tier system, with hate as the worst; Image: Podcaster Matt Walsh is sitting in front of a bookshelf and brick wall; Theme: Direct, blunt; Image: Warm, earthy, rustic colors to foster message connection and relatability	62	43
12. Indifference to Human Life is Worse Than a Hate Crime	10:50	11:43	Words: Indifference to human life, such as mass shooters, school shooters, serial killers, worse than hate crime; Image: Podcaster Matt Walsh is sitting in front of a bookshelf and brick wall; Theme: Persuasive, serious; Image: Warm, earthy, rustic colors to foster message connection and relatability	63	44

Figure 18 Stimulus video 2B – Segment 8: Black Male Attack on White Male
(0m23s to 0m43s)

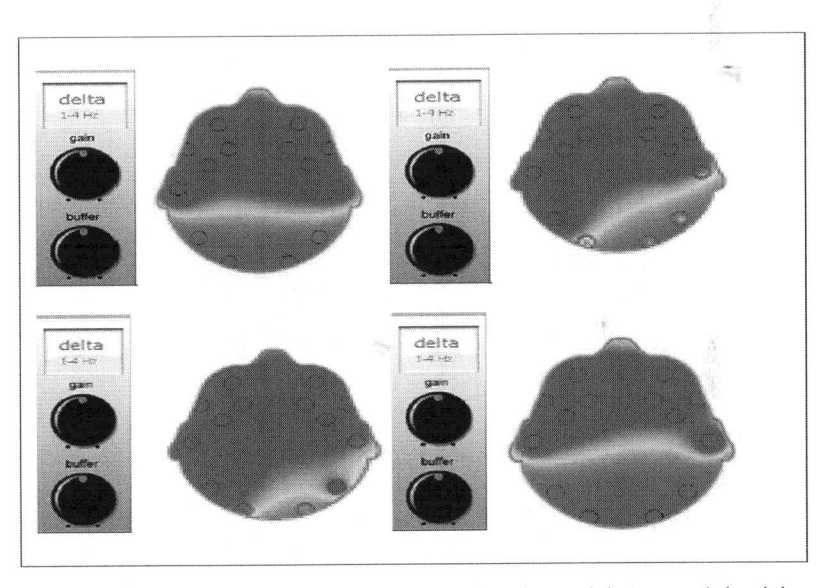

Figure 19 Sample of four randomly selected study participants and the delta
activity imaging results for stimulus video 1B – Segment 8: Black Male Attack
on White Male (0m23s to 0m43s)

Charismatic Leader/Authority

In Table 11 we report the content analytic findings for the right-wing/alt-right
Charismatic Authority/Leader stimulus video, which is an expose by *The
Atlantic*, that includes an interview with white supremacist and alt-right leader
Richard Spencer.

Table 11 Stimulus 3B: Rebranding white nationalism: Inside Richard Spencer's alt-right (Charismatic Authority/Leader)

Segment Label	Time Start	Time End	Elements	# of Study Participants	Average E_A
13. Make America White Again/Trump Energized the Alt-Right	0:11	0:16	Words: Make America white again, Trump energized the Alt-right; Image: White nationalist speaker and author, Richard Spencer is off camera giving an interview then cuts to him sitting in a chair in an obvious hotel room; Theme/Imagery: Direct, matter of fact, neutral tones, the imagery emphasizes the conveyance of information	48	36
14. The Jewish Question/Women Shouldn't Be Allowed to Vote	5:00	6:22	Words: Finally came to understand the Jewish question, and that was difficult because I didn't want to become an anti-Semite because that's the biggest right-wing cliché; segment ends with, Women shouldn't be allowed to vote because it breaks down the entire political system; Image: Richard Spencer at a podium introduces white supremacist YouTuber, Millennial Woes. The segment features him discussing his theories. Theme/Imagery: Busy, with clashing colorful tones, stands in stark visual contrast to Spencer's more sedate segments	47	37

15. Revive Roman Empire, Create A Safe Space for all Europeans	7:51	8:03	Words: Have a safe space for all Europeans around the world; Image: Richard Spencer is sitting in a chair in an obvious hotel room; Theme/Imagery: Direct, matter of fact, even upbeat and jovial at points, neutral tones	45	39
16. Nonwhites Need Us and Not the Other Way Around	9:31	10:11	Words: It is only normal again, when we as Europeans are great again; Image: Richard Spencer at a podium speaking to a ballroom full of people; Theme: Inflammatory, bullish, defiant, rallies and invigorates the group to a standing ovation.	48	38

This video features the use of the Charismatic Authority/Leader as its propaganda device. In the 11min 8s video we identified four segments where there is significant arousal and significant delta activity among the majority of study participants. The highest Average E_A is recorded for the segment titled *Revive the Roman Empire/Create a Safe Space for All Europeans* (Average $E_A = 39$). This particular segment features Richard Spencer sitting in a chair in a hotel room discussing the need for there to be a haven for whites free from targeted violence and reverse discrimination.

The lowest Average E_A score is recorded for the segment titled *Make America White Again/Trump Energized the Alt-Right* (Average $E_A = 36$), which is where Richard Spencer discusses the need to abandon the Republican party, and how the election of Trump helped foster the new alt-right movement. Another segment that reports a strong measure of arousal (Average $E_A = 38$) is that of the segment titled *Nonwhites Need Us, Not the Other Way* Around (Figure 20). This segment features the image of Richard Spencer at a podium speaking to a ballroom full of people (mostly white males), about how the world order of white supremacy is best for whites and non-whites. Figure 21 provides an example of significant delta wave activity for a sample of four randomly selected study participants while viewing Segment 16 (*Nonwhites Need Us, Not the Other Way Around*) of the stimulus video. The combined presence of high levels of arousal with significant delta wave activity indicates an empathetic response during the denoted segments.

Figure 20 Stimulus video 3B – Segment 16: Nonwhites Need Us and Not the Other Way Around (9m31s to 10m11s)

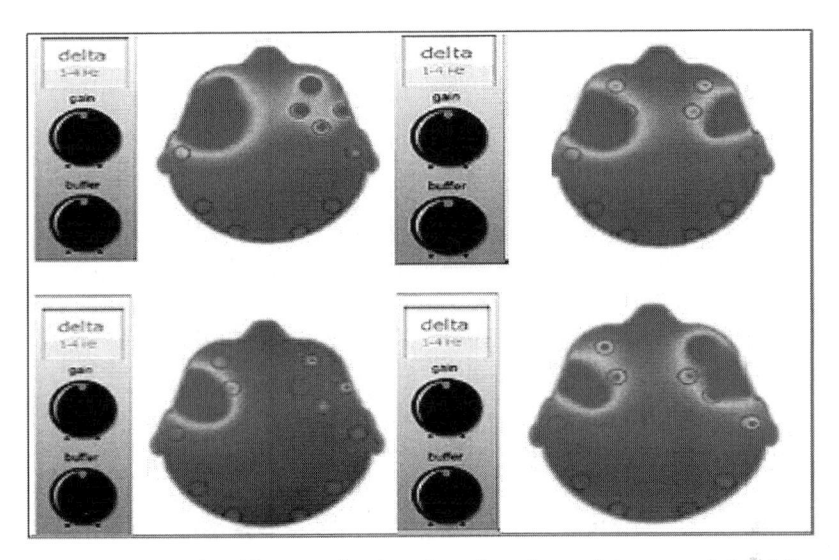

Figure 21 Sample of four randomly selected study participants and the delta activity imaging results for stimulus video 3B – Segment 16: Nonwhites Need Us and Not the Other Way Around (9m31s to 10m11s)

5.4 Discussion of Findings

Across the two studies, the analyses reveal that the use of specific propaganda messaging techniques have the ability to invoke an empathetic response in an experimental setting. Building upon this finding, I assert that when incited within an individual with an already vulnerable preexisting belief system, empathy can remove psychological resistance, thus facilitating the process of radicalization and increasing the potential for terrorism and violent extremism. Among the three types of terrorist and extremist messaging observed, Victim Portrayals evoke the strongest empathetic neural response, while Charismatic Authority/Leader incites the weakest empathetic neural response. Narratives appear to produce an intermediate empathetic neural response.

Looking at Study One first, there are several key findings. First, although all of the study participants would be considered out-group members to the victims (i.e. Western, non-Muslims) in the Victim Portrayal stimulus video, the level of empathetic response for the majority of the participants was significant. When evaluating participants' neural activation in response to the audiovisual stimuli for victim portrayal, we noted that the most salient imagery and rhetorical themes to evoke the strongest and most frequent empathetic responses were those that reflected pain, victimization, and the most vulnerable members of society (i.e. children and the elderly).

For the Narrative stimulus, the findings reveal that for a majority of the study participants, they registered empathetic responses to specific narrative propaganda elements that portrayed ISIS as righteous and strong – with one exception, which I will discuss toward the end of this section. While the participants' responses to the Narrative stimulus were not as significant, in comparison to their responses to the Victim Portrayal stimulus, it is important to note that the study subjects were empathetically responsive to the propaganda messages they viewed.

Finally, for the Charismatic Leader stimulus video, the findings indicate that for certain messages that a majority of the study participants were empathetically responsive. At the same time; however, the findings for this stimulus type were notably weaker in comparison to that of the Victim Portrayal and Narrative stimuli. These findings can likely be attributed to the in-group out-group dynamic. It is entirely likely that the al-Shabaab leader may be charismatic, empathetic, and persuasive to an East African, sub-Saharan African, or Muslim audience, but not to a U.S. audience. And while there was gender, racial and ethnic diversity among the study participants, the lack of national origin and religious diversity, could explain why there was a weak empathetic response to the Charismatic Leader messaging; and that in the absence of significant emotive elements, like those presented in the Victim Portrayal stimulus video, it was perhaps difficult for the study participants to empathize with the leader and his message. With that said, there is one notable exception to the findings here, which is also applicable to the Narrative findings, which I noted previously.

For both message types (Narrative and Charismatic Leader), when themes of victimization and pain were featured in the segment (see Table 6 and 8),[32] there was an observable increase in the number of respondents that reported an empathetic response. Similarly, there was an observable increase in the level of empathetic arousal among the study participants.

This is a key finding because it illustrates that themes of victimization can be used effectively and strategically by terrorist and extremist groups as a radicalization tool by triggering empathetic neural pathways.

Turning now to Study Two, the overall findings are consistent with the findings from those of Study One, in the sense that Victim Portrayals produced the strongest empathetic response, Charismatic Leader elicited the weakest empathetic response, while Narratives evoked an intermediate empathetic response. There are two things that are important about the findings from Study Two. First, as expected, given the racial and ethnic diversity of the study sample, the

---

[32] The referenced segments found in Table 6 and Table 8 are denoted by an asterisk (*)

overall levels of empathetic response, in comparison to the responses from Study One, were significantly lower, in both the number of participants, as well as the level of empathetic arousal.

Several of the study participants, upon completion of the experiment, discussed their disapproval of the content featured in the stimulus videos from Study Two, and noted many of the statements were personally offensive. The study subjects recognized the nature of the research experiment, and did not take issue with viewing the material, but rather " . . . [that] there are people still out here . . . .[in the U.S.], who say things like this, and believe it too" (Study Participant X). The comments of Study Participant X reflect the sentiments of several of the study participants; therefore, I am not surprised that the number of study participants who registered an empathetic response to the messages presented in Study Two was comparatively low in relation to Study One. Nonetheless, despite this tension, the second key finding from this study is all that more important when considering the inherent aversion the study participants had to the stimulus videos in Study Two.

Similar to the findings from Study One, when the participants were exposed to the Victim Portrayal messaging type in Study Two, despite the in-group out-group tension, the level of empathetic response was significant. A substantial majority of the participants registered empathetic responses to several thematic segments presented in the stimulus video, and while the number of participants and the level of empathetic arousal was comparatively lower than the findings from Study One (for Victim Portrayal), the overall trend that these combined findings point to is still noteworthy; the implications of which, will be discussed in greater detail in Section 6.

6 Conclusion: The Neuropolitics of Terrorism and Extremism

Current assessments of terrorism trends indicate that the radical Islamic terrorist threat to the United States remains historically low (Doxsee and Adler, 2024), while the threat from right-wing extremists is at an all-time high. Similarly, across Europe, the alarming ascent of right-wing extremism mirrors that of the domestic challenges facing the United States (Prem, 2024). While outside of the United States, and the nations of the European Union, radical Islamic terrorism continues to threaten global stability, given the recent attacks in Israel, Russia, and the Houthi attacks against U.S. military targets in Yemen (Burke, 2023). Undoubtedly, terrorism and extremism represent a key international security priority. That is why understanding the mechanisms that underlie the radicalization process, which give rise to terrorism and extremism, is an important undertaking.

6.1 What Can We Learn from This Study?

Foremost, one of the key contributions this research makes to the field of terrorism studies is that it helps advance the burgeoning sub-area of neuropolitics or political neuroscience. At the time of this writing, *Inside the Radicalized Mind* and the newly released *The Political Brain* (Qvortrup, 2024) appear to be the only monographs that engage in applied neuropolitics research on political violence.[33] Qvortrup uses fMRI brain imaging technology to explain how political polarization affects one's brain and can influence one's political behavior – nonviolent, but also violent political behavior. *Inside the Radicalized Mind* complements Qvortrup's work and joins it in helping to expand the neuropolitics field, which is in its infancy.

Psychological research has long explored the brain–behavior dynamic in radicalization but is limited by its reliance on behavioral observations and self-report data, which can only hypothesize the role of psychological processes like empathy. While psychology offers a foundational understanding, it doesn't confirm that observed behaviors are truly driven by empathy. Political neuroscience advances this research by providing deeper insights into these brain-behavior connections.

From this study, we now have a better understanding of what is happening to an individual cognitively and emotionally, when they are viewing terrorist and extremist online propaganda materials. As discussed in Section 2 (see Section 2.3.6), from the experiments of cognitive psychologist, Emile Bruneau (2016) and the experimental research of Feddes et al. (2015), we gain insight into the central role empathy plays in the radicalization process and how disparate levels of empathy toward both an out-group and the in-group can, on the one hand, contribute to one's radicalization, but, on the other, can also discourage radicalization.

The findings of this study seem to support the position of Bruneau (2016) and Feddes et al. (2015), in that the stimulus video segments, which produced the highest level of empathetic arousal among the study participants, were segments that featured either in-group victimization (see Table 6 and Table 10) or out-group victimization (see Table 7 and Table 8). The conclusion here is that empathy can be effectively manipulated to either promote or prevent

---

[33] Of note is *Vulnerable Minds: The Neuropolitics of Divided Societies* by Liya Yu (Columbia University Press, 2022). This book builds upon neuroscientific studies to advance a neuropolitical framework to account for discrimination, racism, xenophobia, and dehumanization. Yu's book is groundbreaking, and her analysis challenges our current understanding that "othering" is a learned behavior. *Inside the Radicalized Mind* is informed by Yu's research and builds upon it as well, but Yu's book falls outside the scope of applied neuropolitics, as it is purely theoretical.

radicalization. At the same time, the relationship between in-group and out-group empathy and radicalization does not exist within a vacuum. As I point out in the discussion of my *Cognitive-Emotive Model of Radicalization* in Section 2, empathetic arousal can be stimulated in an experimental setting and never lead to radicalization because the individual lacks a preexisting belief system that would make them vulnerable to empathetic persuasion. Furthermore, empathetic arousal must be generated over multiple settings to have the conditioning effect that results in radicalization, which is not what occurs in an experimental setting that involves a onetime exposure. In other words, an individual may empathize with the imagery, rhetoric, and message they are exposed to, but without a preexisting belief system that is susceptible to empathetic persuasion, and in the absence of frequent and sustained message exposure, radicalization would be highly unlikely. Consequently, empathy is just one factor that plays a role in the radicalization process, albeit it an important one, that we're only beginning to understand.

In addition to highlighting and elevating the importance of empathy, this research helps elucidate Kruglanski et al.'s (2019, 2022b) 3 N Model (the Need, the Network, and the Narrative). While that was never the original goal or intent of this experimental study, in working through the framework of the 3 N Model it became clear that these three conditions operate in collaboration. This study simply identifies one way in which the 3 N Model is applicable, whereby in-group empathy is the motivating Need, the internet is the Network, and, in the case of the findings from this research, propaganda messaging based upon victim portrayals is the salient Narrative. From this standpoint, I conclude that when these three factors are aligned, it increases the risk for radicalization.

So, at the opening of this section, I ask the question, *What Can We Learn from This Study?* And my overarching answer is that we've learned how empathy can be manipulated to encourage or discourage radicalization, which from a counter-radicalization perspective, this is an important finding, because we have a clearer sense of how to design counter-radicalization messages that can be disseminated across the internet with a high likelihood of effectiveness.

6.2 What Do We Still Want To Know?

While we've gained insight into empathy's role in radicalization, many questions remain unanswered. As we expand political neuroscience and explore interdisciplinary approaches, I want to highlight considerations that could address this study's limitations and advance brain–behavior research on radicalization and beyond.

One of this study's limitations is that I focus solely on observing empathetic arousal. However, brain imaging technologies, such as EEG, fMRI, and fNIRS, are capable of detecting the neural basis for a variety of emotions, including happiness, sadness, contentment, amusement, surprise, fear, anger, and even aggression. It would be interesting to gather data on whether a stimulus video is able to arouse empathy and anger, concurrently. In the case of Study Two, where participants expressed displeasure with the stimulus video content, even while empathizing with some of the themes, had I collected data on secondary emotions, such as anger, surprise, aggression, or fear, I could have developed a more nuanced picture of participants' responses.

Also, it would be useful to identify the source of one's empathy in order to measure the levels of empathy a person is experiencing toward an out-group subject versus an in-group subject. Currently, there is no way to capture this distinction using brain imaging technologies; however, in the future, a post-experiment questionnaire could help us get closer to making this distinction. Although a post-experiment survey has its limitations given that it relies upon self-report data, it still would provide us with useful information that we are currently lacking.

Another weakness is this study's instrumentation. Like with any experimental instrument, using EEG alone means we only have one source of data to draw upon. EEG has its advantages over other brain imaging instruments in that it is far less expensive than fMRI and MEG, and even most fNIRS systems, it is easily portable, and can be used on a variety of subjects, including infants. However, it is limited in its ability to capture signals in deeper regions of the brain in comparison to MEG and fMRI, and even fNIRS, the latter of which has better localization of brain signals than EEG and is less sensitive to "noise" from participant movement. When weighing the advantages and disadvantages of the various instruments, using an integrated EEG-fNIRS system would overcome some of the limitations of using EEG alone, while also maintaining the advantage of being easily portable, and still cost-effective. There are several studies that use an integrated EEG-fNIRS system, so that is something I want to explore in the future.

Given that we now have a better understanding of how empathy can be aroused, and subsequently that it can function as a protective factor, in the sense that it could protect an individual from the risk of radicalization, then one immediate next step is to observe whether participants experience empathetic arousal when exposed to counter-radicalization stimulus videos. In a recent study on how to prevent online radicalization, the authors conclude, there seems to be a lack of emotional appeal for many of the counter-narratives that are devised and constructed online, especially those that are more direct and targeted toward terrorist content . . . .violent extremist [and terrorist] narratives are successful because they tap into, and seemingly confirm, existing beliefs of anxieties. The narratives that terrorist groups offer are highly emotional, and therefore the counter-narratives need to reflect this same principle (Zeiger and Gyte, 2021, p. 375).[34]

Given the statements of Zeiger and Gyte (2021), which echo those of Ferguson (2016), and other scholars, there is a clear need to develop more effective counter-messages that operate along similar empathetic emotional pathways as extremist and terrorist messages.

Conducting such an experiment would not only serve to bolster the findings from this study, but also the study findings from earlier research that first identified the centrality of empathy to the radicalization process (Feddes et al., 2015; Bruneau, 2016). More importantly, if we can establish that when individuals are exposed to certain counter-radicalization messages that evoke empathy, that the message is equally or even more persuasive to the receiver than certain extremist messages, then that would lay the foundation for the development of counter-radicalization video campaigns that could then be launched across a number of social media platforms to help mitigate online radicalization.

6.3 Element Conclusion

This Element provides an analysis of how internet-based videos have the potential to arouse empathy and generate radical-persuasive outcomes among individuals exposed to right-wing (alt-right) extremist and radical Islamic terrorist messaging. In conducting the analysis, this study accounts for the individualized process of radicalization and the saliency of one's existing belief system, while also highlighting the importance of the message construction itself.

Given the findings of this Element, this research has important security policy implications, because it suggests that if empathy can be aroused in response to extremist videos, thereby increasing the likelihood of the video's persuasive effectiveness, then it is equally possible to develop effectual online counter-messaging strategies if the message features empathetic elements that resonate with the target audience.

---

[34] See also, p. 13 of Ferguson, Kate. (2016). "Countering Violent Extremism through Media and Communication Strategies: A Review of the Evidence," Partnership for Conflict, Crime & Security Research (PaCCS). www.paccsresearch.org.uk/wp-content/uploads/2016/03/Countering-Violent-Extremism-Through-Media-and-Communication-Strategies-.pdf.

References

Alexander, I. D. and Poch, R. K. (2017) *Innovative learning and teaching: Experiments across the disciplines*. University of Minnesota Libraries. http://open.lib.umn.edu/innovativeteaching.

Alkan Härtwig, E., Aust, S., Heekeren, H. R., and Heuser, I. (2020) "No words for feelings? Not only for my own: Diminished emotional empathic ability in alexithymia," *Frontiers in Behavioral Neuroscience*, 14, p. 112.

Allely, C. S. (2020) *The psychology of extreme violence: A case study approach to serial homicide, mass shooting, school shooting, and lone-actor terrorism*. Routledge.

Allendorfer, W. H. and Herring, S. C. (2015) "ISIS vs. the US government: A war of online video propaganda," *First Monday*, 20(12), https://firstmon day.org/ojs/index.php/fm/article/view/6336/5165.

Alsobrook, J. P. 2nd and Pauls, D. L. (2000) "Genetics and violence," *Child and Adolescent Psychiatric Clinics of North America*, 9(4), pp. 765–776.

Amble, J. C. (2012) "Combating terrorism in the new media environment," *Studies in Conflict & Terrorism*, 35(5), pp. 339–353.

Antilla, L. (2010) "Self-censorship and science: A geographical review of media coverage of climate tipping points," *Public Understanding of Science*, 19(2), pp. 240–256.

Atran, S. (2021) "Psychology of transnational terrorism and extreme political conflict," *Annual Review of Psychology*, 72(1), pp. 471–501.

Azam, J.-P. and Delacroix, A. (2006) "Aid and the delegated fight against terrorism," *Review of Development Economics*, 10(2), pp. 330–344.

Azam, J.-P. and Thelen, V. (2008). "The roles of foreign aid and education in the war on terror," *Public Choice*, 135, pp. 375–397, https://doi.org/10.1007/s11127-007-9268-4.

Azam, J.-P. and Thelen, V. (2018) *Fighting terrorism at source: Using foreign aid to delegate global security*. Edward Elgar Publishing.

Baele, S. J., Boyd, K. A., and Coan, T. G. (Eds.). (2020). *ISIS propaganda: A full-spectrum extremist message*. Oxford University Press.

Bagozzi, R. P. and Moore, D. J. (1994) "Public service advertisements: Emotions and empathy guide prosocial behavior," *The Journal of Marketing*, 56, pp. 56–70.

Baines, P. R., O'Shaughnessy, N. J., Moloney, K., et al. (2010) "The dark side of political marketing: Islamist propaganda, reversal theory and British Muslims," *European Journal of Marketing*, 44(3–4), pp. 478–495.

Baker, A. (2016) "Active learning with interactive videos: Creating student-guided learning materials," *Journal of Library & Information Services in Distance Learning*, 10(3–4), pp. 79–87.

Baker, L. A., Raine, A., Liu, J., and Jacobson, K. C. (2008) "Differential genetic and environmental influences on reactive and proactive aggression in children," *Journal of Abnormal Child Psychology*, 36, pp. 1265–1278.

Baldner, C. and McGinley, J. J. (2014) "Correlational and exploratory factor analyses (EFA) of commonly used empathy questionnaires: New insights," *Motivation and Emotion*, 38(5), pp. 727–744.

Baliga, S. and Sjöström, T. (2009) "Decoding terror," *Econometrica*, 77(1), pp. 27–59.

Barkun, M. (1990) "Racist apocalypse: Millennialism on the far right," *American Studies*, 31(2), pp. 121–140.

Bartels, A. and Zeki, S. (2004) "Functional brain mapping during free viewing of natural scenes," *Human Brain Mapping*, 21(2), pp. 75–85.

Becker, J. C., Tausch, N., and Wagner, U. (2011) "Emotional consequences of collective action participation: Differentiating self-directed and outgroup-directed emotions," *Personality and Social Psychology Bulletin*, 37(12), pp. 1587–1598.

Beevor, E. (2017) "Coercive radicalization: Charismatic authority and the internal strategies of ISIS and the Lord's Resistance Army," *Studies in Conflict & Terrorism*, 40(6), pp. 496–521.

Benford, R. D. and Snow, D. A. (2000) "Framing processes and social movements: An overview and assessment," *Annual Review of Sociology*, 26, pp. 611–639.

Benton-Peterka, D. and Benton, B. (2023) "Online radicalization case study of a mass shooting: The Payton Gendron manifesto," *Journal for Deradicalization*, 35, pp. 1–32.

Berg, R., Brand, A., Grant, J., Kirk, J. S., and Zimmerman, T. (2014) "Leveraging recorded mini-lectures to increase student learning," *Online Classroom*. www.csusb.edu/sites/default/files/upload/file/Leveraging_Recorded_Mini-Lectures_to_Inc.pdf.

Berrebi, C. (2007) "Evidence about the link between education, poverty, and terrorism among Palestinians," *Peace Economics, Peace Science and Public Policy*, 13(1), pp. 1–36.

Bezdjian, S., Raine, A., Baker, L. A., and Lynam, D. R. (2011) "Psychopathic personality in children: Genetic and environmental contributions," *Psychological Medicine*, 41(3), pp. 589–600.

Bilandzic, H. and Busselle, R. (2013) "Narrative persuasion," in Dillard, J. P. and Shen, L. (eds.) *The SAGE handbook of persuasion: Developments in theory and practice.* SAGE, pp. 200–219.

Binder, J. F. and Kenyon, J. (2022). "Terrorism and the internet: How dangerous is online radicalization?," *Frontiers in Psychology,* p. 13, https://doi.org/10.3389/fpsyg.2022.997390.

Blair, R. J. (2018) "Traits of empathy and anger: Implications for psychopathy and other disorders associated with aggression," *Philosophical Transactions of the Royal Society B: Biological Sciences,* 373(1744), pp. 1–8.

Blair, G., Fair, C. C., Malhotra, N., and Shapiro, J. N. (2013) "Poverty and support for militant politics: Evidence from Pakistan," *American Journal of Political Science,* 57(1), pp. 30–48.

Borum, R. (2004) *Psychology of terrorism.* University of South Florida.

(2011). "Radicalization into violent extremism I: A review of social science theories," *Journal of Strategic Security,* 4(4), pp. 7–36, http://www.jstor.org/stable/26463910.

(2014) "Psychological vulnerabilities and propensities for involvement in violent extremism," *Behavioral Sciences & the Law,* 32(3), pp. 286–305.

Boyns, D. and Ballard, J. D. (2004) "Developing a sociological theory for the empirical understanding of terrorism," *The American Sociologist,* 35(2), pp. 5–25.

Braddock, K. H. (2012) *Fighting words: The persuasive effect of online extremist narratives on the radicalization process* (Doctoral dissertation, The Pennsylvania State University). Retrieved from https://etda.libraries.psu.edu/files/final_submissions/7610.

Braddock, K. and Dillard, J. (2016) "Meta-analytic evidence for the persuasive effect of narratives on beliefs, attitudes, intentions, and behaviors," *Communication Monographs,* 83(4), pp. 446–467.

Brame, C. J. (2016) "Effective educational videos: Principles and guidelines for maximizing student learning from video content," *CBE-Life Sciences Education,* 15(4), es6.

Branscombe, N. R. and Wann, D. L. (1994) "Collective self-esteem consequences of outgroup derogation when a valued social identity is on trial," *European Journal of Social Psychology,* 24(6), pp. 641–657.

Bruneau, E. (2016) "Understanding the terrorist mind," *Cerebrum: The Dana Forum on Brain Science,* 2016, Article Cer-13–16. November, https://www.dana.org/article/understanding-the-terrorist-mind/.

Bruneau, E. G., Cikara, M., and Saxe, R. (2017) "Parochial empathy predicts reduced altruism and the endorsement of passive harm," *Social Psychological and Personality Science,* 8, pp. 934–942.

Buckels, E. and Trapnell, P. (2013) "Disgust facilitates out-group dehumanization," *Group Processes & Intergroup Relations*, 16, pp. 771–780.

Burke, J. (2023, October 18) "Attacks across Europe put Islamist extremism back in spotlight," *The Guardian*. www.theguardian.com/world/2023/oct/17/attacks-across-europe-put-islamist-extremism-back-in-spotlight.

Cahill, M., Migacheva, K., Taylor, J., et al. (2021) *Understanding online hate speech as a motivator and predictor of hate crime*. Los Angeles, California, 2017–2018 (ICPSR 37470) [Data set]. National Archive of Criminal Justice Data, https://doi.org/10.3886/ICPSR37470.v1.

Campbell, R. and Babrow, A. (2004) "The role of empathy in responses to persuasive risk communication: Overcoming resistance to HIV prevention messages," *Health Communication*, 16, pp. 159–182.

Canetti, D. (2017) "Emotional distress, conflict ideology, and radicalization," *PS: Political Science & Politics*, 50(4), pp. 940–943.

Carmichael, M., Reid, A.K., and Karpicke, J. D. (2018) *Assessing the impact of educational video on student engagement, critical thinking and learning: The current state of play*. A SAGE White Paper. https://us.sagepub.com/sites/default/files/hevideolearning.pdf.

Carpenter, J. (1997) *Revive us again: The reawakening of American fundamentalism*. Oxford University Press.

Carr, D. (2014) "With videos of killings, ISIS sends medieval message by modern method," *The New York Times*, 7, https://www.nytimes.com/2014/09/08/business/media/with-videos-of-killings-isis-hones-social-media-as-a-weapon.html.

Casebeer, W. and Russell, J. (2005) "Storytelling and terrorism: Towards a comprehensive 'counter-narrative strategy'," *Strategic Insights*, 4(3), https://ntrl.ntis.gov/NTRL/dashboard/searchResults/titleDetail/ADA521449.xhtml.

Caspi, A., McClay, J., Moffitt, T. E., et al. (2002) "Role of genotype in the cycle of violence in maltreated children," *Science (New York, N.Y.)*, 297(5582), pp. 851–854.

Cavanaugh, M. M. (2012) "Theories of violence: Social science perspectives," *Journal of Human Behavior in the Social Environment*, 22(5), pp. 607–618.

Chadee, D., Chadee, M., Brewster, D., and Surette, R. (2017) "Copycat crime dynamics: The interplay of empathy, narrative persuasion and risk with likelihood to commit future criminality," *Psychology of Popular Media Culture*, 6(2), pp. 142–158. https://doi.org/10.1037/ppm0000079.

Chaiken, S., Wood, W., and Eagly, A. H. (1996) "Principles of persuasion," in Higgins, E. T. and Kruglanski, A. W. (eds.) *Social psychology: Handbook of basic principles*. Guilford Press, pp. 702–742.

Cho, J., Boyle, M. P., Keum, H., et al. (2003) "Media, terrorism, and emotionality: Emotional differences in media content and public reactions to the September 11th terrorist attacks," *Journal of Broadcasting & Electronic Media*, 47(3), pp. 309–327.

Chory-Assad, R. and Cicchirillo, V. (2005) "Empathy and affective orientation as predictors of identification with television characters," *Communication Research Reports*, 22, pp. 151–156.

Christmann, K. (2012) *Preventing religious radicalisation and violent extremism: A systematic review of the research evidence.* Youth Justice Board.

Chrysikou, E. G. and Thompson, W. J. (2016) "Assessing cognitive and affective empathy through the interpersonal reactivity index: An argument against a two-factor model," *Assessment*, 23(6), pp. 769–777.

Cialdini, R. B. and Goldstein, N. J. (2004) "Social influence: Compliance and conformity," *Annual Review of Psychology*, 55, pp. 591–621.

Clegg, S. R. (1989) *Frameworks of power.* SAGE.

Clever, L., Schatto-Eckrodt, T., Clever, N. C., and Frischlich, L. (2023) "Behind blue skies: A multimodal automated content analysis of Islamic extremist propaganda on Instagram," *Social Media + Society*, 9(1), 2056305122 1150404.

Cohen, J. (2006) "Audience identification with media characters," in Bryant, J. and Vorderer, P. (eds.) *Psychology of entertainment.* Lawrence Erlbaum Associates, pp. 183–197.

Cohen, T. R. (2008) *The effects of empathy on intergroup conflict and aggression: Examining the dual roles of empathy in fostering positive and negative intergroup relations* (Doctoral dissertation). The University of North Carolina at Chapel Hill.

Cohen, S. J., Johansson, F., Kaati, L., and Mork, J. C. (2016) "Al-Qaeda's propaganda decoded: A psycholinguistic system for detecting variations in terrorism ideology," *Terrorism and Political Violence*, 28(5), pp. 1–30.

Collins, R. (1986) *Weberian sociological theory.* Cambridge University Press.
   (2004) "Rituals of solidarity and security in the wake of terrorist attack," *Sociological Theory*, 22(1), pp. 53–87.

Conway, M. (2016). "Determining the role of the internet in violent extremism and terrorism: Six suggestions for progressing research," *Studies in Conflict & Terrorism*, 40(1), pp. 77–98.

Corman, S. (2011) "Understanding the role of narrative in extremist strategic communication," in Fenstermacher, L. and Canna, S. (eds.) *Countering violent extremism: Scientific methods & strategies.* Air Force Research Laboratory, pp. 36–43.

Coser, L. A. (1956) *The functions of social conflict.* Routledge.

Council of Europe. (n.d.). *Online Hate Speech and Hate Crime – Cyberviolence* – www.coe.int. www.coe.int/en/web/cyberviolence/online-hate-speech-and-hate-crime.

Cozma, S.-G. (2014) "Islamic self-radicalization on the internet: A global process reflected nationally," *Romanian Intelligence Review*, 12, pp. 69–82. www.ceeol.com/search/article-detail?id=68124.

Crenshaw, M. (1998) "The logic of terrorism: Terrorist behavior as a product of strategic choice," in Reich, W. (ed.) *Origins of terrorism: Psychologies, ideologies, theologies, states of mind*. Woodrow Wilson Center Press, pp. 7–24.

(2000) "The psychology of terrorism: An agenda for the 21st century," *Political Psychology*, 21(2), pp. 405–420.

(2012) "The causes of terrorism," in Horgan, J. and Braddock, K. (eds.) *Terrorism studies: A reader*. Routledge, pp. 99–114.

Crilley, K. (2001) "Information warfare: New battle fields terrorists, propaganda and the Internet," *Aslib Proceedings*, 53(7), pp. 294–300.

Crockett, M. J., Clark, L., Hauser, M. D., and Robbins, T. W. (2010). "Serotonin selectively influences moral judgment and behavior through effects on harm aversion," *Proceedings of the National Academy of Sciences*, 107(40), pp. 17433–17438.

Damasio, A. (2004) "Emotions and feelings," in Manstead, A. (ed.) *Feelings and emotions: The Amsterdam symposium*. Cambridge University Press, pp. 48–58.

Da Silva, C., Kruglanski, A. W., and Pierro, A. (2024) "Significance quest: A meta-analysis on the association between the variables of the 3 N model and violent extremism," *Trauma, Violence, & Abuse*, 25(2), pp. 1184–1200.

DataReportal. (2024, October) Digital 2024 October Global Statshot Report. https://datareportal.com/reports/digital-2024-october-global-statshot.

Davis, M. H. (1980) "A multidimensional approach to individual differences in empathy," *JSAS Catalog of Selected Documents in Psychology*, 10(85), https://www.uv.es/~friasnav/Davis_1980.pdf.

Davis, M. H. (1983) "Measuring individual differences in empathy: Evidence for a multidimensional approach," *Journal of Personality and Social Psychology*, 44(1), pp. 113–126.

Davis, M. H. (1996) *Empathy: A social psychological approach*. Westview Press.

Davis, R. L. and O'Neill, P. (2016) "The hate crimes reporting gap: Low numbers keep tensions high," *The Police Chief*, 83. www.policechiefmagazine.org/the-hate-crimes/.

Dawson, L. L. (2002) "Crises of charismatic legitimacy and violent behavior in new religious movements," in Bromley, D. G. and Melton, J. G. (eds.) *Cults, religion and violence.* Cambridge University Press, pp. 80–101.

(2006) "Psychopathologies and the attribution of charisma: A critical introduction to the psychology of charisma and the explanation of violence in new religious movements," *Nova Religio,* 10(2), pp. 3–28.

Dean, G. (2014) *Neurocognitive risk assessment for the early detection of violent extremists.* Springer Briefs in Criminology.

Decety, J. and Jackson, P. (2004) "The functional architecture of human empathy," *Behavioral and Cognitive Neuroscience Reviews,* 3, pp. 71–100.

(2006) "A social neuroscience perspective on empathy," *Current Directions in Psychological Science,* 15, pp. 54–58.

Decety, J. and Lamm, C. (2006) "Human empathy through the lens of social neuroscience," *Scientific World Journal,* 6, pp. 1146–1163.

Decety, J. and Yoder, K. J. (2016) "Empathy and motivation for justice: Cognitive empathy and concern, but not emotional empathy, predict sensitivity to injustice for others," *Social Neuroscience,* 11(1), pp. 1–14.

Decety, J. and Workman, C. I. (2017) "The effects of poverty on the brain: A neurocognitive perspective," *Trends in Cognitive Sciences,* 21(5), pp. 344–360.

Decety, J. and Yoder, K. J. (2017) "The emerging social neuroscience of justice motivation," *Trends in Cognitive Sciences,* 21(1), pp. 6–14.

DeCorte, K., Buysse, A., Verhofstadt, L. L., et al. (2007) "Measuring empathic tendencies: Reliability and validity of the Dutch version of the interpersonal reactivity index," *Psychologica Belgica,* 47(4), p. 235.

Delić, D. (2022) *20 Online hate crime statistics and facts for 2024.* ProPrivacy.com. https://proprivacy.com/blog/online-hate-crime-statistics-and-facts-2022.

Della Porta, D. and LaFree, G. (2012) "Guest editorial: Processes of radicalization and de-radicalization," *International Journal of Conflict and Violence (IJCV),* 6(1), pp. 4–10.

Deloughery, K., King, R. D., and Asal, V. (2012) "Close cousins or distant relatives? The relationship between terrorism and hate crime," *Crime & Delinquency,* 58(5), pp. 663–688.

DeZavala, A. G., Cislak, A., and Wesołowska, E. (2010) "Political conservatism, need for cognitive closure, and intergroup hostility," *Political Psychology,* 31(4), pp. 521–541.

Domestic Terrorism Prevention Act of 2019 (2019) U.S. Senate Bill S.894. U.S. Senate, 116th Congress, 1st Session. www.congress.gov/116/bills/s894/BILLS-116s894is.xml.

Donoghue, T., Dominguez, J., and Voytek, B. (2020) "Electrophysiological frequency band ratio measures conflate periodic and aperiodic neural activity," *Eneuro*, 7(6), pp. 1–14.

Doosje, B., Moghaddam, F. M., Kruglanski, A. W., et al. (2016) "Terrorism, radicalization and de-radicalization," *Current Opinion in Psychology*, 11, pp. 79–84.

Doxsee, C. and Adler, L. (2024, February 9) "Asked and answered: Global terrorism threat assessment 2024," *Center for Strategic and International Studies (CSIS)*. www.csis.org/analysis/asked-and-answered-global-terror ism-threat-assessment-2024.

Dreißigacker, A., Müller, P., Isenhardt, A., and Schemel, J. (2024) "Online hate speech victimization: Consequences for victims' feelings of insecurity," *Crime Science*, 13(4), https://doi.org/10.1186/s40163-024-00204-y.

Durkheim, E. (1984) *The division of labor in society* (W. D. Halls, Trans.). Free Press. (Original work published 1893)

Durkheim, E. (1995) *The elementary forms of religious life* (K. E. Fields, Trans.). Free Press. (Original work published 1912).

Eisenberg, N. and Miller, P. A. (1987) "The relation of empathy to prosocial and related behaviors," *Psychological Bulletin*, 101(1), pp. 91–119.

Elmasry, M. H. and el-Nawawy, M. (2020) "Can a non-Muslim mass shooter be a 'terrorist'?: A comparative content analysis of the Las Vegas and Orlando shootings," *Journalism Practice*, 14(7), pp. 863–879.

Enders, W. and Sandler, T. (2011). *The political economy of terrorism* (2nd ed.). Cambridge University Press.

Enders, W. and Sandler, T. (2012) "The economics of terrorism and counter-terrorism: What matters and is rational-choice theory helpful?" *Journal of Conflict Resolution*, 56(2), pp. 214–231.

Espiritu, A. (2004) "Racial diversity and hate crime incidents," *The Social Science Journal*, 41(2), pp. 197–208.

Europol. (2016). European Union terrorism situation and trend report (TE-SAT) 2016. European Police Office. Available at: https://www.europol.europa .eu/cms/sites/default/files/documents/europol_tesat_2016.pdf.

Falk, E. B., Rameson, L., Berkman, E. T., et al. (2010) "The neural correlates of persuasion: A common network across cultures and media," *Journal of Cognitive Neuroscience*, 22(11), pp. 2447–2459.

"Far-Right Terrorism Increase in the West Explained" (2021, September 7) *Institute for economics & peace*. www.visionofhumanity.org/explainer-far-right-terrorism-in-the-west/.

Farwell, J. P. (2014) "The media strategy of ISIS," *Survival*, 56(6), pp. 49–55.

Fearon, J. D. and Laitin, D. D. (2003) "Ethnicity, insurgency, and civil war," *American Political Science Review*, 97(1), pp. 75–90.

Feddes, A. R., Mann, L., and Doosje, B. (2015) "Increasing self-esteem and empathy to prevent violent radicalization: A longitudinal quantitative evaluation of a resilience training focused on adolescents with a dual identity," *Journal of Applied Social Psychology*, 45(7), pp. 400–411.

Ferguson, K. (2016) *Countering violent extremism through media and communication strategies: A review of the evidence.* Partnership for Conflict, Crime & Security Research (PaCCS). www.paccsresearch.org.uk/wp-content/uploads/2016/03/Countering-Violent-Extremism-Through-Media-and-Communication-Strategies-.pdf.

Ferguson, C. J. and Beaver, K. M. (2009) "Natural born killers: The genetic origins of extreme violence," *Aggression and Violent Behavior*, 14(5), pp. 286–294.

Fisogni, P. (2019) "Cyber terrorism and self-radicalization – Emergent phenomena of onlife age: An essay through the general system theory," *International Journal of Cyber Warfare and Terrorism*, 9(3), pp. 21–35.

Freytag, A., Krüger, J. J., Meierrieks, D., and Schneider, F. G. (2009). "The origins of terrorism: Cross-country estimates on socio-economic determinants of terrorism," *Jena Economic, Research Papers*, No. 2009-009. https://www.econstor.eu/bitstream/10419/31767/1/593202562.PDF.

Freytag, A., Krüger, J. J., Meierrieks, D., and Schneider, F. (2011) "The origins of terrorism: Cross-country estimates on socio-economic determinants of terrorism," *European Journal of Political Economy*, 27(1), pp. S5–S16.

Gambhir, H. (2014) *Dabiq: The strategic messaging of the Islamic State.* Institute for the Study of War.

Ganor, B. (2002) "Defining terrorism: Is one man's terrorist another man's freedom fighter?" *Police Practice and Research*, 3(4), pp. 287–304.

Garcia-Arocena, D. (2015) *The genetics of violent behavior.* The Jackson Laboratory. www.jax.org/news-and-insights/jax-blog/2015/december/the-genetics-of-violent-behavior.

Gasser, T., Verleger, R., Bächer, P., and Sroka, L. (1988) "Development of the EEG of school-age children and adolescents: I. Analysis of band power," *Electroencephalography and Clinical Neurophysiology*, 69(2), pp. 91–99.

Geelhoed, F. (2011) "Fundamentalism," in Ross, J. I. (ed.) *Religion and violence: An encyclopedia of faith and conflict from antiquity to the present.* M.E. Sharpe, p. 368.

Gendron, A. (2017) "The call to jihad: Charismatic preachers and the internet," *Studies in Conflict & Terrorism*, 40(1), pp. 44–61.

Gill, P. (2015) *Lone-actor terrorists: A behavioral analysis.* Routledge.

Gill, P., Corner, E., Conway, M., et al. (2017). "Terrorist use of the Internet by the numbers: Quantifying behaviors, patterns, and processes," *Criminology & Public Policy*, 16(1), pp. 99–117.

Glenn, A. L. and Raine, A. (2014) *Psychopathy: An introduction to biological findings and their implications* (Vol. 1). NYU Press.

Goldie, P. (1999) "How we think of others' emotions," *Mind & Language*, 14(4), pp. 394–423.

Gonzalez, J. (2020, June 13) "To boost higher-order thinking, try curation," *Cult of Pedagogy*. www.cultofpedagogy.com/curation/.

Gunning, J. (2007) "A case for critical terrorism studies?" *Government and Opposition*, 42(3), pp. 363–393.

Guo, P. J., Kim, J., and Rubin, R. (2014) "How video production affects student engagement: An empirical study of MOOC videos," *Proceedings of the First ACM Conference on Learning @ Scale Conference*, pp. 41–50.

Gurr, T. R. (1970) *Why men rebel*. Princeton University Press.

Hadden, B. W., Øverup, C. S., and Knee, C. R. (2014) "Removing the ego: Need fulfillment, self-image goals, and self-presentation," *Self and Identity*, 13(3), pp. 274–293.

Hamid, N., Pretus, C., Atran, S., et al. (2019) "Neuroimaging 'Will to Fight' for sacred values: An empirical case study with supporters of an Al Qaeda associate," *Royal Society Open Science*, 6(6), https://royalsocietypublishing .org/doi/10.1098/rsos.181585.

Hamid, N. and Ariza, C. (2022). Offline versus online radicalization: Which is the bigger threat? Tracing outcomes of 439 jihadist terrorists between 2014–2021 in 8 Western countries. GNET report. Available at: https://gnet-research.org/ wp-content/uploads/2022/02/GNET-Report-Offline-Versus-Online-Radicalization.pdf.

Hamm, M. S. and Spaaij, R. F. J. (2017) *The age of lone wolf terrorism*. Columbia University Press.

Hancock, J. B., Beaver, D. I., Chung, C. K., et al. (2010) "Social language processing: A framework for analyzing the communication of terrorists and authoritarian regimes," *Behavioral Sciences of Terrorism and Political Aggression*, 2(2), pp. 108–132.

Hartleb, F. (2020) *Lone wolves: The new terrorism of right-wing single actors*. Springer International.

Hasson, U., Nir, Y., Levy, I., Fuhrmann, G., and Malach, R. (2004) "Intersubject synchronization of cortical activity during natural vision," *Science*, 303(5664), pp. 1634–1640.

Heath-Kelly, C. (2013) "Counter-terrorism and the counterfactual: Producing the 'radicalisation' discourse and the UK Prevent strategy," *The British Journal of Politics and International Relations*, 15(3), pp. 394–415.

Herring, S. C. (2004) "Content analysis for new media: Rethinking the paradigm," in *New research for new media: Innovative research methodologies symposium working papers and readings*. University of Minnesota School of Journalism and Mass Communication, pp. 47–66, https://homes.luddy.indiana.edu/herring/newmedia.pdf.

(2009) "Web content analysis: Expanding the paradigm," in Noor, H. H. and Schmid, R. F. J. (eds.) *International handbook of internet research*. Springer Netherlands, pp. 233–249.

Hess, G. D. and Blomberg, S. B. (2008) "From (no) butter to guns? Understanding the economic role in terrorism," in Keefer, P. and Loayza, N. (eds.) *Terrorism, economic development, and political openness*. Cambridge University Press, pp. 83–115.

Hewstone, M. and Cairns, E. (2001) "Social psychology and intergroup conflict," in Chirot, D. and Seligman, M. (eds.) *Ethnopolitical warfare: Causes, consequences, and possible solutions*. American Psychological Association, pp. 319–342.

Hewstone, M., Cairns, E., Voci, A., et al. (2004). "Intergroup contact in a divided society: Challenging segregation in Northern Ireland," In *Social psychology of inclusion and exclusion*. Psychology Press, pp. 283–310.

Himichi, T. and Nomura, M. (2015) "Modulation of empathy in the left ventrolateral prefrontal cortex facilitates altruistic behavior: An fNIRS study," *Journal of Integrative Neuroscience*, 14(2), pp. 207–222.

Hoffman, B. (2006) *Inside terrorism* (Revised and Expanded ed.). Columbia University Press.

Hoffman, S. (2023, October 31) "Interpersonal reactivity index – Psychology," *Eckerd College*. www.eckerd.edu/psychology/iri/.

Hofmann, D. C. (2015) "Quantifying and qualifying charisma: A theoretical framework for measuring the presence of charismatic authority in terrorist groups," *Studies in Conflict & Terrorism*, 38(9), pp. 710–733.

(2016) "The influence of charismatic authority on operational strategies and attack outcomes of terrorist groups," *Journal of Strategic Security*, 9(2), pp. 14–44.

Hofmann, D. C. and Dawson, L. L. (2014) "The neglected role of charismatic authority in the study of terrorist groups and radicalization," *Studies in Conflict & Terrorism*, 37(4), pp. 348–368.

Hollewell, G. F. and Longpré, N. (2022) "Radicalization in the social media era: Understanding the relationship between self-radicalization and the internet," *International Journal of Offender Therapy and Comparative Criminology*, 66(8), pp. 896–913.

Horgan, J. (2014) *The psychology of terrorism* (2nd ed.). Taylor and Francis.

(2024) *Terrorist minds: The psychology of violent extremism from Al-Qaeda to the far right*. Columbia University Press.

Howard, T. (2008) "Revisiting state failure: Developing a causal model of state failure based upon theoretical insight," *Civil Wars*, 10(2), pp. 125–146.

(2010a) "Failed states and the spread of terrorism in sub-Saharan Africa," *Studies in Conflict and Terrorism*, 33(11), pp. 960–988.

(2010b) *The tragedy of failure: Evaluating state failure and its impact on the spread of refugees, terrorism, and war*. ABC-CLIO.

(2014) *Failed states and the origins of violence: A comparative analysis of state failure as a root cause of terrorism and political violence*. Routledge.

Howard, T., Poston, B., and Benning, S. D. (2019) "The neurocognitive process of digital radicalization: A theoretical model and analytical framework," *Journal for Deradicalization*, Summer (19), pp. 122–148, https://journals.sfu.ca/jd/index.php/jd/issue/view/21.

Howard, T., Poston, B., and Lopez, A. (2022) "Extremist radicalization in the virtual era: Analyzing the neurocognitive process of online radicalization," *Studies in Conflict and Terrorism*, 47(8), pp. 862–887, https://doi.org/10.1080/1057610X.2021.2016558.

Hummell, W. and Huntress, K. (1949). *The analysis of propaganda*. Holt, Rinehart, and Winston, p. 2.

Huppert, T. J., Hoge, R. D., Diamond, S. G., Franceschini, M. A., and Boas, D. A. (2006). "A temporal comparison of BOLD, ASL, and NIRS hemodynamic responses to motor stimuli in adult humans," *NeuroImage*, 29(2), pp. 368–382. https://doi.org/10.1016/j.neuroimage.2005.08.065.

Husna, S. (2020, July) "Into the mind of terrorist & violent-extremist: A neuroscience perspective & review on radicalization," in *Annual International Conference on Social Sciences and Humanities (AICOSH 2020)*. Atlantis Press, pp. 1–5.

Ilardi, G. J. (2001) "Redefining the issues: The future of terrorism research and the search for empathy," in Silke, A. (ed.) *Research on terrorism: Trends, achievements & failures*. Frank Cass, pp. 16–35.

Inan, Y. (2007). "Cyber terrorism: The new kind of terrorism," *Journal of Information Technology Impact*, 7(2), pp. 93–104.

Influs, M., Hackman, J., Feldman, R., and Hendler, T. (2019) "A social neuroscience approach to conflict resolution: Dialogue intervention to Israeli and

Palestinian youth impacts oxytocin and empathy," *Social Neuroscience*, 14(4), pp. 378–389, https://doi.org/10.1080/17470919.2018.1544329.

Ito, T. A. and Kubota, J. T. (2023, January 18) "7.1: Social neuroscience," *Social Sci LibreTexts*. https://socialsci.libretexts.org/Bookshelves/Psychology/ Introductory_Psychology/Psychology_as_a_Biological_Science_(Noba)/ 07%3A_Social/7.01%3A_Social_Neuroscience.

(2024) "Social neuroscience," in Biswas-Diener, R. and Diener, E. (eds.) *Noba textbook series: Psychology*. DEF. https://nobaproject.com/modules/ social-neuroscience.

Jääskeläinen, I. P., Koskentalo, K., Balk, M. H., et al. (2008) "Inter-subject synchronization of prefrontal cortex hemodynamic activity during natural viewing," *The Open Neuroimaging Journal*, 2(1), 14–19.

Jabbi, M., Swart, M., and Keysers, C. (2007) "Empathy for positive and negative emotions in the gustatory cortex," *NeuroImage*, 34(4), pp. 1744–1753.

Jackson, R. (2007) "The core commitments of critical terrorism studies," *European Political Science*, 6(3), pp. 244–251.

Jasko, K., Szastok, M., Grzymała-Moszczyńska, J., Maj, M., and Kruglanski, A. W. (2019) "Rebel with a cause: Personal significance from political activism predicts willingness to self-sacrifice," *Journal of Social Issues*, 75(1), pp. 314–349.

Jasper, J. (1998) "The emotions of protest: Affective and reactive emotions in and around social movements," *Sociological Forum*, 13(3), pp. 397–424.

Jasper, J. and Poulsen, J. (1995) "Recruiting strangers and friends: Moral shocks and social networks in animal rights and anti-nuclear protests," *Social Problems*, 42(4), pp. 493–512.

Jastorff, J. and Orban, G. A. (2009) "Human functional magnetic resonance imaging reveals separation and integration of shape and motion cues in biological motion processing," *The Journal of Neuroscience*, 29(22), pp. 7315–7329.

Jenkins, J. C. (1983) "Resource mobilization theory and the study of social movements," *Annual Review of Sociology*, 9(1), pp. 527–553.

Jensen, M., James, P., and Tinsley, H. (2015) Profiles of individual radicalization in the United States: An empirical assessment of domestic radicalization. START, College Park, Maryland. www.start.umd.edu/pubs/PIRUS% 20Fact%20Sheet_Jan%202015.pdf.

Jensen, M., James, P., Yates, E., and Tinsley, H. (2018) *The use of social media by United States extremists*. START, College Park, Maryland. www.start.umd .edu/pubs/START_PIRUS_UseOfSocialMediaByUSExtremists_Research Brief_July2018.pdf.

Johnson, J. (2018) "The self-radicalization of white men: 'Fake news' and the affective networking of paranoia," *Communication, Culture & Critique*, 11(1), pp. 100–115.

Johnson-Laird, P. N. and Oatley, K. (2000) "Cognitive and social construction in emotions," in Lewis, M. and Haviland-Jones, J. M. (eds.), *Handbook of emotions* (2nd ed.), Guilford Press, pp. 458–475.

Kanwisher, N. and Yovel, G. (2006) "The fusiform face area: A cortical region specialized for the perception of faces," *Philosophical Transactions of the Royal Society B: Biological Sciences*, 361(1476), pp. 2109–2128.

Karimova, E. D., Smolskaya, D. V., and Naratkina, A. A. (2023) "Activity of the mirror neuron system in people with depressive symptomatology," *Neuroscience and Behavioral Physiology*, 53(7), pp. 1202–1209.

Kauttonen, J., Hlushchuk, Y., and Tikka, P. (2015) "Optimizing methods for linking cinematic features to fMRI data," *NeuroImage*, 110, pp. 136–148.

Kenyon, J., Binder, J., and Baker-Beall, C. (2021) Exploring the role of the Internet in radicalisation and offending of convicted extremists. Ministry of Justice. Available at: https://assets.publishing.service.gov.uk/media/614088c2e90e070442fbdde2/exploring-role-internet-radicalisation.pdf.

Kenyon, J., Binder, J., and Baker-Beall, C. (2022). "Understanding the role of the internet in the process of radicalisation: An analysis of convicted extremists in England and Wales," *Studies in Conflict & Terrorism*, 47(12), pp. 1747–1771. https://doi.org/10.1080/1057610X.2022.2065902.

Khalil, J., Horgan, J., and Zeuthen, M. (2022) "The Attitudes-Behaviors Corrective (ABC) model of violent extremism," *Terrorism and Political Violence*, 34(3), pp. 425–450.

Kilner, J. M. and Lemon, R. N. (2013) "What we know currently about mirror neurons," *Current Biology*, 23(23), pp. R1057–R1062.

Klasen, M., Wolf, D., Eisner, P. et al. (2018) "Neural networks underlying trait aggression depend on MAOA gene alleles," *Brain Structure & Function*, 223(2), pp. 873–881.

Knight, A. (2007) "Jihad and cross-cultural media: Osama bin Laden as reported in the Asian press," *Pacific Journalism Review*, 13(2), pp. 155–174.

Knight, S., Woodward, K., and Lancaster, G. (2017) *Violent versus non-violent actors: An empirical study of different types of extremism*. American Psychological Association.

Knight, S., Keatley, D., and Woodward, K. (2019) "Comparing the different behavioral outcomes of extremism: A comparison of violent and non-violent extremists, acting alone or as part of a group," *Studies in Conflict & Terrorism*, 45(8), pp. 682–703.

Koomen, W. and Van Der Pligt, J. (2016) *The psychology of radicalization and terrorism*. Routledge.

Kosiński, J., Szklanny, K., Wieczorkowska, A., and Wichrowski, M. (2018) "An analysis of game-related emotions using EMOTIV EPOC," in *2018 Federated conference on computer science and information systems (FedCSIS)*. IEEE, pp. 913–917.

Kraidy, M. (2017) "The projectilic image: Islamic State's digital visual warfare and global networked affect," *Media, Culture & Society*, 39(8), pp. 1194–1209.

Krakowski, M. (2003) "Violence and serotonin: Influence of impulse control, affect regulation, and social functioning," *The Journal of Neuropsychiatry and Clinical Neurosciences*, 15(3), pp. 294–305.

Krueger, A. (2007) *What makes a terrorist: Economics and the roots of terrorism*. Princeton University Press.

Krueger, A. and Malečková, J. (2003) "Education, poverty, and terrorism: Is there a causal connection?" *Journal of Economic Perspectives*, 17(4), pp. 119–144.

Kruglanski, A. W., Jasko, K., Webber, D., Chernikova, M., and Molinario, E. (2018) "The making of violent extremists," *Review of General Psychology*, 22(1), pp. 107–120.

Kruglanski, A. W., Gunaratna, R., and Bélanger, J. J. (2019) *The three pillars of radicalization: Needs, narratives, and networks*. Oxford University Press.

Kruglanski, A. W. and Ellenberg, M. (2020) "The quest for personal significance and ideological violence," *AJOB Neuroscience*, 11(4), pp. 285–287.

Kruglanski, A. W., Kopetz, C., and Szumowska, E. (2022a) *The psychology of extremism: A motivational perspective*. Routledge.

Kruglanski, A. W., Molinario, E., Jasko, K., et al. (2022b) "Significance-quest theory," *Perspectives on Psychological Science*, 17(4), pp. 1050–1071.

Kundnani, A. (2012) "Radicalisation: The journey of a concept," *Race & Class*, 54(2), pp. 3–25.

Kurrild-Klitgaard, P., Justesen, M. K., and Klemmensen, R. (2006) "The political economy of freedom, democracy and transnational terrorism," *Public Choice*, 128(1/2), pp. 289–315.

Lai, B. (2007). "'Draining the Swamp': An empirical examination of the production of international terrorism, 1968–1998," *Conflict Management and Peace Science*, 24(4), pp. 297–310. http://www.jstor.org/stable/26275248.

Lankinen, K., Saari, J., Hari, R., and Koskinen, M. (2014) "Intersubject consistency of cortical MEG signals during movie viewing," *NeuroImage*, 92, pp. 217–224.

Large, M. E., Cavina-Pratesi, C., Vilis, T., and Culham, J. C. (2008) "The neural correlates of change detection in the face perception network," *Neuropsychologia*, 46(8), pp. 2169–2176.

Lazarus, R. (1991) *Emotion and adaptation*. Oxford University Press.

Lee, M. F. and Simms, H. (2008) "American millenarianism and violence: Origins and expression," *Journal for the Study of Radicalism*, 1(2), pp. 107–127.

Lee, J., Kim, T. W., Lee, C. S., and Koo, C. (2022) "Integrated approach to evaluating the effect of indoor CO2 concentration on human cognitive performance and neural responses in office environment," *Journal of Management in Engineering*, 38(1), https://ascelibrary.org/doi/abs/10.1061/%28ASCE%29ME.1943-5479.0000993.

Leitch, S. and Pickering, P. (2022) *Rethinking social media and extremism*. ANU Press.

Lemieux, A. F. (2006) "Social psychological approaches to understanding and preventing terrorism: Toward an interdisciplinary perspective," *Journal of Security Education*, 1(4), pp. 75–83.

Lemieux, A. F. and Pratto, F. (2003) "Poverty and prejudice," in Carr, S. and Sloan, T. (eds.) *Poverty and psychology: Emergent critical practice*. Kluwer Academic, pp. 147–162.

Lewis, D. (2019) "The rise of the self-radicalized lone wolf terrorist," *Vision of Humanity*. www.visionofhumanity.org/increase-in-self-radicalised-lone-wolf-attackers/.

Lupu, Y., Radford, B., Spry, E., and Thomas, K. (2023) "Offline events and online hate," *PLOS ONE*, 18(1), p. e0278511, https://doi.org/10.1371/journal.pone.0278511.

Majdandžić, J., Amashaufer, S., Hummer, A., Windischberger, C., and Lamm, C. (2016) "The selfless mind: How prefrontal involvement in mentalizing with similar and dissimilar others shapes empathy and pro-social behavior," *Cognition*, 157, pp. 24–38.

Maogoto, J. N. (2003) "War on the enemy: Self-defence and state-sponsored terrorism," *Melbourne Journal of International Law*, 4(2), pp. 406–438.

Maskaliūnaitė, A. (2015) "Exploring the theories of radicalization," *International Studies: Interdisciplinary Political and Cultural Journal (IS)*, 17(1), pp. 9–26.

Maslow, A. H. (1954) *Motivation and personality*. Harpers.

Matar, D. (2015) "Hassan Nasrallah: The cultivation of image and language in the making of a charismatic leader," *Communication, Culture & Critique*, 8(3), pp. 433–447.

Matsumoto, D., Frank, M., and Hwang, H. (2015) "The role of intergroup emotions in political violence," *Current Directions in Psychological Science*, 24(5), pp. 369–373.

McCarthy, J. D. and Zald, M. N. (1977) "Resource mobilization and social movements: A partial theory," *American Journal of Sociology*, 82(6), pp. 1212–1241.

McCauley, C. and Moskalenko, S. (2008) "Mechanisms of political radicalization: Pathways toward terrorism," *Terrorism and Political Violence*, 20(3), pp. 415–433.

McCauley, C. and Moskalenko, S. (2010) "Recent US thinking about terrorism and counterterrorism: Baby steps towards a dynamic view of asymmetric conflict," *Terrorism and Political Violence*, 22(4), pp. 641–657.

McCauley, C. and Moskalenko, S. (2011) *Friction: How radicalization happens to them and us*. Oxford University Press.

McCauley, C. and Moskalenko, S. (2017a) "Lone wolf terrorists: What motivates them?" *Defence Procurement International* (March). www.defence procurementinternational.com/features/land/lone-wolf-terrorist-attacks-on-the-west.

McCauley, C. and Moskalenko, S. (2017b) "Understanding political radicalization: The two-pyramids model," *The American Psychologist*, 72(3), pp. 205–216.

McDermott, R., Tingley, D., Cowden, J., Frazzetto, G., and Johnson, D. D. P. (2009) "Monoamine oxidase A gene (MAOA) predicts behavioral aggression following provocation," *Proceedings of the National Academy of Sciences*, 106(7), pp. 2118–2123.

McDowell-Smith, A., Speckhard, A., and Yayla, A. S. (2017) "Beating ISIS in the digital space: Focus testing ISIS defector counter-narrative videos with American college students," *Journal for Deradicalization*, 10, pp. 50–76.

McLernon, F., Cairns, E., Hewstone, M., and Smith, R. (2003) "Memories of recent conflict and forgiveness in Northern Ireland," in Cairns, E. and Roe, M. D. (eds.) *The role of memory in ethnic conflict*. Palgrave Macmillan UK, pp. 125–143.

Miller, L. (2006a) "The terrorist mind: I. A psychological and political analysis," *International Journal of Offender Therapy and Comparative Criminology*, 50(2), pp. 121–138.

Miller, L. (2006b) "The terrorist mind: II. Typologies, psychopathologies, and practical guidelines for investigation," *International Journal of Offender Therapy and Comparative Criminology*, 50(3), pp. 255–268.

Moghaddam, F. M. (2005) "The staircase to terrorism: A psychological exploration," *The American Psychologist*, 60(2), pp. 161–169.

Moghaddam, F. M. and Marsella, A. J. (2004) *Understanding terrorism: Psychosocial roots, consequences, and interventions.* American Psychological Association.

Morris, T. (2012) "Extracting and networking emotions in extremist propaganda," in *Intelligence and Security Informatics Conference (EISIC), 2012 European.* IEEE, pp. 3–8, https://doi.org/10.1109/EISIC.2012.16.

Müller, M. and Pillay, N. (2024) "Cognitive flexibility in urban yellow mongooses, *Cynictis penicillata*," *Animal Cognition*, 27(1), Article 14. https://doi.org/10.1007/s10071-024-01839-9.

Nasser-Eddine, M., Garnham, B., Agostino, K., and Caluya, G. (2011) *Countering violent extremism (CVE) literature review counter terrorism and security technology centre.* Australian Government, Department of Defence. http://dspace.dsto.defence.gov.au/dspace/bitstream/1947/10150/1/DSTO-TR-2522%20PR.pdf.

Newman, E. (2006) "Exploring the 'root causes' of terrorism," *Studies in Conflict & Terrorism*, 29(8), pp. 749–772.

Neumann, P. R. (2013) "The trouble with radicalization," *International Affairs*, 89(4), pp. 873–893.

Neumann, D. L. and Westbury, H. R. (2011) "The psychophysiological measurement of empathy," in Decety, J. (ed.) *The Oxford handbook of the development of empathy.* Oxford University Press, pp. 119–142.

Neumann, D. L., Chan, R. C. K., Wang, Y., and Boyle, G. J. (2015) "Measures of empathy: Self-report, behavioral, and neuroscientific approaches," in Boyle, G. J., Saklofske, D. H., and Matthews, G. (eds.) *Measures of personality and social psychological constructs.* Academic Press, pp. 257–289.

Obaidi, M., Anjum, G., Bierwiaczonek, K., et al. (2023) "Cultural threat perceptions predict violent extremism via need for cognitive closure," *Proceedings of the National Academy of Sciences of the United States of America*, 120(20), https://www.pnas.org/doi/epub/10.1073/pnas.2213874120.

Oberschall, A. (2004) "Explaining terrorism: The contribution of collective action theory," *Sociological Theory*, 22(1), pp. 26–37.

Ofcom and Traverse (2023) *Qualitative research into the impact of online hate: Final report.* www.ofcom.org.uk/__data/assets/pdf_file/0020/252740/qual-research-impact-of-online-hate.pdf.

Office of the National Security Advisor (2015) *National security strategy.* https://obamawhitehouse.archives.gov/sites/default/files/docs/2015_national_security_strategy_2.pdf.

O'Loughlin, B., Boudeau, C., and Hoskins, A. (2011) "Distancing the extraordinary: Audience understandings of discourses of 'radicalization'," *Continuum: Journal of Media & Cultural Studies*, 25(2), pp. 153–164.

Oosterwijk, S., Lindquist, K. A., Anderson, E. C., and Barrett, L. F. (2012) "States of mind: Emotions, body feelings, and thoughts share distributed neural networks," *NeuroImage*, 62(3), pp. 2110–2128.

Oxford University Press (2010) *Oxford English dictionary* (3rd ed.). Oxford University Press.

Pape, R. (2005) *Dying to win: The strategic logic of suicide terrorism*. Random House.

Pariser, E. (2011). *The filter bubble: What the internet is hiding from you*. Penguin Press.

Parker, A. (2020) "Self-radicalization in the United States via social media and other online forums," in Khasru, S. M. (ed.) *The digital age, cyber space, and social media: The challenges of security & radicalization*. IPAG, pp. 31–41. https://www.researchgate.net/publication/341830466_The_Digital_Age_ Cyber_Space_and_Social_Media_The_Challenges_of_Security_Radicalizati on_edited_by_Syed_M_Khasru_Institute_for_Policy_Advocacy_and_Gover nance_IAPG_Allison_Wylde_Chapter_13_Resilience_Rev.

Payne, K. (2009). *Winning the battle of ideas: Propaganda, ideology, and terror*. Praeger Security International.

Peelen, M. V. and Downing, P. E. (2005) "Within-subject reproducibility of category-specific visual activation with functional MRI," *Human Brain Mapping*, 25(4), pp. 402–408.

Petrosyan, A. (2022) "Impact of online hate and harassment in the U.S. 2020," *Statista*. www.statista.com/statistics/971876/societal-impact-of-online-hate-harassment-usa/.

Piazza, J. (2007) "Draining the swamp: Democracy promotion, state failure, and terrorism in 19 Middle Eastern countries," *Studies in Conflict & Terrorism*, 30(6), pp. 521–539.

Piazza, J. A. (2008). "Incubators of terror: Do failed and failing states promote transnational terrorism?" *International Studies Quarterly*, 52(3), pp. 469–488.

Pisiou, D. (2012) *Islamist radicalization in Europe: An occupational change process*. Routledge.

Post, J. M. (2007) *The mind of the terrorist: The psychology of terrorism from the IRA to Al-Qaeda* (1st ed.). Palgrave Macmillan.

Power, S. (2002) *A problem from hell: America and the age of genocide*. Perennial.

Prem, A. S. (2024, February 6) "The creeping ascent of the far-right in mainstream European politics and how to stop it," *LSE Undergraduate Political Review*. https://blogs.lse.ac.uk/lseupr/2024/02/06/the-creeping-ascent-of-the-far-right-in-mainstream-european-politics-and-how-to-stop-it/ (Accessed: August 21, 2024).

Preston, S. and de Waal, F. (2002) "Empathy: Its ultimate and proximate bases," *Behavioral and Brain Sciences*, 25(1), pp. 1–72.

Pretus, C., Hamid, N., Sheikh, H., et al. (2018) "Neural and behavioral correlates of sacred values and vulnerability to violent extremism," *Frontiers in Psychology*, 9, Article 2024.

Qvortrup, M. (2024). *The political brain: The emergence of neuropolitics*. Central European University Press.

Rajakumar, V. (2013) "Alternative perspectives on the radicalization of home-grown and 'leaderless' terrorists," *Counter Terrorist Trends and Analyses*, 5(8), pp. 20–22.

Ramirez, R. and Vamvakousis, Z. (2012) "Detecting emotion from EEG signals using the Emotiv EPOC device," in He, Y., Wu, Z., and Lin, W. (eds.) *Brain informatics: Proceedings of the 2012 international conference on brain informatics*. Springer, pp. 62–70.

Rapoport, D. (2022) *Waves of global terrorism: From 1879 to the present*. Columbia University Press.

Reed, A., Whittaker, J., and Votta, F. (2019). "Radical filter bubbles: Social media personalisation algorithms and extremist content," *Internet Policy Review*, 8(4).

Reiss, D., Leve, L. D., and Neiderhiser, J. M. (2013) "How genes and the social environment moderate each other," *American Journal of Public Health*, 103(Suppl 1), pp. S111–S121.

Relia, K., Li, Z., Cook, S. H., and Chunara, R (2019) "Race, ethnicity and national origin-based discrimination in social media and hate crimes across 100 U.S. cities," *arXiv.Org*. January 3. https://arxiv.org/abs/1902.00119.

Rieger, D., Frischlich, L., and Bente, G. (2013) "Propaganda 2.0: Psychological effects of right-wing and Islamic extremist internet videos," *Media and Communication*, 1(1), pp. 39–50.

(2020) "Dealing with the dark side: The effects of right-wing extremist and Islamist extremist propaganda from a social identity perspective," *Media, War & Conflict*, 13(3), pp. 280–299.

Rifkind, G. (2018) *The psychology of political extremism: What would Sigmund Freud have thought about Islamic State?* Routledge, pp. 55–74.

Robinson, M. D. and Dauber, C. E. (2019) "Grading the quality of ISIS videos: A metric for assessing the technical sophistication of digital video propaganda," *Studies in Conflict & Terrorism*, 42(1–2), pp. 70–87.

Roessing, T. and Siebert, S. (2006) "Perception and assessment of left- and right-wing extremism by public opinion: An experimental study," in *59th WAPOR Annual conference proceedings*. WAPOR.

Rrustemi, A. (2020) *Measuring the impact of the lifestory approach on preventing and countering violent extremism.* Hague Centre for Strategic Studies.

Saby, J. and Marshall, P. (2012) "The utility of EEG band power analysis in the study of infancy and early childhood," *Developmental Neuropsychology,* 37(3), pp. 253–273.

Sageman, M. (2004) *Understanding terror networks.* University of Pennsylvania Press.

(2008) *Leaderless Jihad: Terror networks in the twenty-first century.* University of Pennsylvania Press.

Saha, K., Chandrasekharan, E., and De Choudhury, M. (2019) "Prevalence and psychological effects of hateful speech in online college communities," in *Proceedings of the 10th ACM conference on web science (WebSci '19).* Association for Computing Machinery, New York, NY, USA, pp. 255–264. https://doi.org/10.1145/3292522.3326032.

Salem, A., Reid, E., and Chen, H. (2008) "Multimedia content coding and analysis: Unraveling the content of jihadi extremist groups' videos," *Studies in Conflict & Terrorism,* 31(7), pp. 605–626.

Sandholtz, N., Langston, L., and Planty, M. (2013) *Hate crime victimization, 2003–2011: Special report* (NCJ 241291). Bureau of Justice Statistics, U.S. Department of Justice. www.bjs.gov/content/pub/pdf/hcv0311.pdf (Accessed: August 21, 2024).

Savage, S. and Fearon, P. (2021) "Increasing cognitive complexity and meta-awareness among at-risk youth in Bosnia-Herzegovina in order to reduce risk of extremism and interethnic tension," *Peace and Conflict: Journal of Peace Psychology,* 27(2), pp. 225–239.

Saxe, R., Xiao, D. K., Kovacs, G., Perrett, D. I., and Kanwisher, N. (2004) "A region of right posterior superior temporal sulcus responds to observed intentional actions," *Neuropsychologia,* 42(11), pp. 1435–1446.

Schmid, A. (2013) *Radicalization, de-radicalization, counter-radicalization: A conceptual discussion and literature review.* ICCT Research Paper. International Centre for Counterterrorism.

Schumann, S., Salman, N. L., Clemmow, C., Gill, P. (2022) "Does cognitive inflexibility predict violent extremist behaviour intentions? A registered direct replication report of Zmigrod, Rentfrow, & Robbins, 2019," *Legal and Criminological Psychology,* 27, pp. 329–353, https://doi.org/10.1111/lcrp.12201.

Schweppe, J. (2021) "What is a hate crime?" *Cogent Social Sciences,* 7(1), Article 1902643.

Shane, S. and Hubbard, B. (2014) "ISIS displaying a deft command of varied media," *The New York Times,* 31 Aug. 2014, p. A1(L). Gale General

OneFile, link.gale.com/apps/doc/A380813054/ITOF?u=unlv_main&sid= bookmark-ITOF&xid=5520b3fc (Accessed January 22, 2025).

Shafi, N. (2021) "The neuroscience of terrorism: A neuroscientific approach to understanding cognitive-behavioral traits of violent extremists," *The New School Psychology Bulletin*, 18(1), pp. 1–18. www.nspb.net/index.php/ nspb/article/view/335 (Accessed: August 21, 2024).

Shen, L. (2010) "Mitigating psychological reactance: The role of message-induced empathy in persuasion," *Human Communication Research*, 36(3), pp. 397–422.

(2014) "Antecedents to psychological reactance: The impact of threat, message frame, and choice," *Health Communication*, 30(10), pp. 1–11.

(2019) "Features of empathy-arousing strategic messages," *Health Communication*, 34(11), pp. 1329–1339. https://doi.org/10.1080/ 10410236.2018.1485078.

Shen, L. and Seung, S. Y. (2018) "On measures of message elaboration in narrative communication," *Communication Quarterly*, 66(1), pp. 79–95.

Sherif, M. (1966) *In common predicament: Social psychology of intergroup conflict and cooperation.* Houghton-Mifflin.

Shortland, N. D. (2021) *The psychology of terrorism.* Routledge, Taylor & Francis Group.

Sidanius, J. and Pratto, F. (1999) *Social dominance: An intergroup theory of social hierarchy and oppression.* Cambridge University Press.

Silber, M. and Bhatt, A. (2007) *Radicalization in the West: The homegrown threat.* New York Police Department. https://info.publicintelligence.net/ NYPDradicalization.pdf (Accessed: August 21, 2024).

Silke, A. (2003) *Terrorists, victims, and society: Psychological perspectives on terrorism and its consequences.* Wiley.

Simmel, G. (1955) *Conflict and the web of group affiliations* (K. H. Wolff and R. Bendix, Trans.). Free Press. (Original work published 1908).

Singer, T., Seymour, B., O'Doherty, J., et al. (2006) "Empathic neural responses are modulated by the perceived fairness of others," *Nature*, 439(7075), pp. 466–479.

Smith, A. (2010) "Cognitive empathy and emotional empathy in human behavior and evolution," *The Psychological Record*, 56(1), https://www.researchgate .net/publication/46283381_Cognitive_Empathy_and_Emotional_Empathy_ in_Human_Behavior_and_Evolution.

Spaaij, R. (2012) *Understanding lone wolf terrorism: Global patterns, motivations and prevention.* Springer.

Speckhard, A. (2008) "The emergence of female suicide terrorists," *Studies in Conflict & Terrorism*, 31(11), pp. 995–1023.

Springer, N. R. (2009) *Patterns of Radicalization: Identifying the Markers and Warning Signs of Domestic Lone Wolf Terrorists in our Midst* (Master's thesis). Naval Postgraduate School, Monterey, CA. Retrieved from: https://apps.dtic.mil/sti/pdfs/ADA514419.pdf.

Sprinzak, E. (2001) "The lone gunmen," *Foreign Policy*, 127, pp. 72–73.

START (National Consortium for the Study of Terrorism and Responses to Terrorism) (2022) *Global Terrorism Database 1970–2020* [data file]. www.start.umd.edu/gtd.

Staub, E. (1989) *The roots of evil: The origins of genocide and other group violence*. Cambridge University Press.

Staub, E. (2003) *The psychology of good and evil: Why children, adults, and groups help and harm others*. Cambridge University Press.

Steinbach, M. (2016) "ISIL online: Countering terrorist radicalization and recruitment on the internet and social media," *Statement before the Senate Committee on Homeland Security and Governmental Affairs*, July 6. www.fbi.gov/news/testimony/isil-online-countering-terrorist-radic alization-and-recruitment-on-the-internet-and-social-media-   (Accessed: August 21, 2024).

Sternberg, R. (2003) "A duplex theory of hate: Development and application to terrorism, massacres, and genocide," *Review of General Psychology*, 7, pp. 299–328.

Sternberg, R. (2005) "Understanding and combating hate," in Sternberg, R. (ed.) *The psychology of hate*. American Psychological Association, pp. 37–50.

Stremlau, N., McGeer, C., and Straub, M. (2024) "Deciphering digital hate: Assessing the evidence between online speech and offline violence in Africa," *Global Media Journal: German Edition*, 13(2), https://www .globalmediajournal.de/index.php/gmj/article/view/280.

Strindberg, A. (2020) Social identity theory and the study of terrorism and violent extremism. Stockholm: Totalförsvarets forskningsinstitut.

Swisher, S., Martin, A., Ritchie, L., et al. (2016) "Orlando nightclub gunman made Facebook posts, texted his wife during standoff," *The Orlando Sentinel*, June 16. www.orlandosentinel.com/news/pulse-orlando-night club-shooting/os-omar-mateen-thursday-update-20160616-story.html (Accessed: August 21, 2024).

Taarnby, M. (2005) "Recruitment of Islamist terrorists in Europe: Trends and perspectives," *Research Report funded by the Danish Ministry of Justice*, January 14, https://www.investigativeproject.org/documents/testimony/ 58.pdf.

Tabares, A. S. G. and Durán Palacio, N. M. (2021) "The protective role of empathy and emotional self-efficacy in predicting moral disengagement in adolescents separated from illegal armed groups," *Anuario de Psicología Jurídica*, 31(1), pp. 127–136.

Tajfel, H. and Turner, J. (1986) "The social identity theory of intergroup behavior," in Worchel, S. and Austin, W. G. (eds.) *Psychology of intergroup relations*. Nelson Hall, pp. 7–24.

Tausch, N., Becker, J. C., Spears, R., et al. (2011) "Explaining radical group behavior: Developing emotion and efficacy routes to normative and non-normative collective action," *Journal of Personality and Social Psychology*, 101(1), pp. 129–145.

Taylor, D. M. and Moghaddam, F. M. (1994) *Theories of intergroup relations: International social psychological perspectives* (2nd ed.). Praeger.

Taylor, M. and Horgan, J. (2006) "A conceptual framework for addressing psychological process in the development of the terrorist," *Terrorism and Political Violence*, 18(4), pp. 585–601.

The Covenant of the Hamas-Main Points (1988) *Charter of Hamas*. https://irp .fas.org/world/para/docs/880818a.htm (Accessed: August 21, 2024).

Thompson, R. (2011)) "Radicalization and the use of social media," *Journal of Strategic Security*, 4(4), pp. 167–190.

Tiihonen, J., Rautiainen, M. R., Ollila, H. M., et al. (2015). "Genetic background of extreme violent behavior. Molecular psychiatry," 20(6), pp. 786–792. https://doi.org/10.1038/mp.2014.130.

Tilly, C. (2003) *The politics of collective violence*. Cambridge: Cambridge University Press.

Tschantret, J. (2021) "The psychology of right-wing terrorism: A text-based personality analysis," *Psychology of Violence*, 11(2), pp. 113–122.

Turner, J. H. (2009) "The sociology of emotions: Basic theoretical arguments," *Emotion Review*, 1(4), pp. 340–354.

Tuttle Ross, S. (2002). "Understanding propaganda: The epistemic merit model and its application to art," *Journal of Aesthetic Education* 36 (1), pp. 16–30.

Tuvblad, C. and Baker, L. A. (2011) "Human aggression across the lifespan: Genetic propensities and environmental moderators," *Advances in Genetics*, 75, pp. 171–214.

Tyler, T. R. (1994) "Psychological models of the justice motive: Antecedents of distributive and procedural justice," *Journal of Personality and Social Psychology*, 67(5), pp. 850–863.

United Nations Office on Drugs and Crime (UNODC) (2018) Counter-terrorism module two-key issues: Radicalization and violent extremism.

www.unodc.org/e4j/zh/terrorism/module-2/key-issues/radicalization-violent-extremism.html (Accessed: August 21, 2024).

Vacca, J. R. (2019) *Online terrorist propaganda, recruitment, and radicalization*. CRC Press.

Van den Bos, K. (2018) *Why people radicalize: How unfairness judgments are used to fuel radical beliefs, extremist behaviors, and terrorism*. Oxford University Press.

Vanderwert, R. E. and Nelson, C. A. (2014) "The use of near-infrared spectroscopy in the study of typical and atypical development," *Neuroimage*, 85, pp. 264–271.

Vertigans, S. (2011) *The sociology of terrorism: People, places and processes* (1st ed.). Routledge.

Vertigans, S. (2013). *The sociology of terrorism: People, places and processes*. Routledge.

Victoroff, J. (2005) "The mind of the terrorist: A review and critique of psychological approaches," *Journal of Conflict Resolution*, 49(1), pp. 3–42.

von Behr, I., Reding, A., Edwards, C., and Gribbon, L. (2013) "Radicalization in the digital era: The use of the internet in 15 cases of terrorism and extremism," RAND Corporation. Retrieved from https://www.rand.org/pubs/research_reports/RR453.html.

Webber, D., Babush, M., Schori-Eyal, N., et al. (2018) "The road to extremism: Field and experimental evidence that significance loss-induced need for closure fosters radicalization," *Journal of Personality and Social Psychology*, 114(2), pp. 270–285.

Weber, M. (1946) *From Max Weber: Essays in sociology*. Oxford University Press.

Welch, T. (2018) "Theology, heroism, justice, and fear: An analysis of ISIS propaganda magazines *Dabiq* and *Rumiyah*," *Dynamics of Asymmetric Conflict*, 11(3), pp. 186–198.

Williams, C. A. (1990) "Bio-psychosocial elements of empathy: A multidimensional model,"," *Issues in Mental Health Nursing*, 11(2), pp. 155–174.

Williams, M. L., Burnap, P., Javed, A., Liu, H., and Ozalp, S. (2020) "Hate in the machine: Anti-Black and anti-Muslim social media posts as predictors of offline racially and religiously aggravated crime," *The British Journal of Criminology*, 60(1), pp. 93–117.

Winkates, J. (2006) "Suicide terrorism: Martyrdom for organizational objectives," *Journal of Third World Studies*, 23(1), pp. 87–115.

Winkler, C., Eldamanhoury, K., Dicker, A., and Lemieux, A. F. (2019) "Images of death and dying in ISIS media: A comparison of English and Arabic print publications," *Media, War & Conflict*, 12(3), pp. 248–262, https:// doi.org/10.1177/1750635217746200.

Winter, C., Neumann, P., Meleagrou-Hitchens, A., et al. (2020) "Online extremism: Research trends in internet activism, radicalization, and counter-strategies," *International Journal of Conflict and Violence (IJCV)*, 14, pp. 1–20.

Wintrobe, R. (2012) *Rational extremism: The political economy of radicalism*. Cambridge University Press.

Wojcieszak, M. and Kim, N. (2016) "How to improve attitudes toward disliked groups: The effects of narrative versus numerical evidence on political persuasion," *Communication Research*, 43(6), pp. 785–809.

Yan, N., Wang, J., Liu, M., et al. (2008) "Designing a brain-computer interface device for neurofeedback using virtual environments," *Medical and Biological Engineering*, 28(3), pp. 167–172.

Yoder, K. J. and Decety, J. (2014) "The good, the bad, and the just: Justice sensitivity predicts neural response during moral evaluation of actions performed by others," *Journal of Neuroscience*, 34(12), pp. 4161–4166.

Yoder, K. J., Ruby, K., Pape, R., and Decety, J. (2020). "EEG distinguishes heroic narratives in ISIS online video propaganda," *Scientific Reports*, 10(1), p. 19593. https://doi.org/10.1038/s41598-020-76711-0.

Zanolie, K. and Crone, E. A. (2018) *Stevens' handbook of experimental psychology and cognitive neuroscience*, *4th Ed.* John Wiley & Sons.

Zeiger, S. and Gyte, J. (2021) "Prevention of radicalization on social media and the internet [book]," in Schmid, A. P. (ed.) *The handbook of terrorism prevention and preparedness*. ICCT Press, pp. 358–360. www.icct.nl/sites/ default/files/2023-01/Chapter-12-Handbook_0.pdf (Accessed: August 21, 2024).

Zheng, W. L. and Lu, B. L. (2015) "Investigating critical frequency bands and channels for EEG-based emotion recognition with deep neural networks," *IEEE Transactions on Autonomous Mental Development*, 7(3), pp. 162–175.

Zhong, W., Cristofori, I., Bulbulia, J., Krueger, F., and Grafman, J. (2017) "Biological and cognitive underpinnings of religious fundamentalism," *Neuropsychologia*, 100, pp. 18–25.

Zillmann, D. (2006) "Empathy: Affective reactivity to others' emotional experiences," in Bryant, J. and Vorderer, P. (eds.) *Psychology of entertainment*. Lawrence Erlbaum, pp. 151–181.

Zmigrod, L. (2020) "The role of cognitive rigidity in political ideologies: Theory, evidence, and future directions," *Current Opinion in Behavioral Sciences*, 34, pp. 34–39.

Zmigrod, L., Rentfrow, P. J., and Robbins, T. W. (2019) "Cognitive inflexibility predicts extremist attitudes," *Frontiers in Psychology*, 10, p. 989.

Cambridge Elements ≡

Experimental Political Science

James N. Druckman

University of Rochester

James N. Druckman is the Martin Brewer Anderson Professor of Political Science at the University of Rochester. He served as an editor for the journals Political Psychology and Public Opinion Quarterly as well as the University of Chicago Press's series in American Politics. He currently is the co-Principal Investigator of Time-sharing Experiments for the Social Sciences (TESS) and sits on the boards of the American National Election Studies, the General Social Survey, and the Russell Sage Foundation. He previously served as President of the American Political Science Association section on Experimental Research and helped oversee the launching of the Journal of Experimental Political Science. He was co-editor of the Cambridge Handbook of Experimental Political Science and Advances in Experimental Political Science. He authored the book Experimental Thinking: A Primer on Social Science Experiments. He is a Fellow of the American Academy of Arts and Sciences and has published approximately 200 articles/book chapters on public opinion, political communication, campaigns, research methods, and other topics.

About the Series

There currently are few outlets for extended works on experimental methodology in political science. The new Experimental Political Science Cambridge Elements series features research on experimental approaches to a given substantive topic, and experimental methods by prominent and upcoming experts in the field.

Cambridge Elements $\equiv$

Experimental Political Science

Printed in the United States
by Baker & Taylor Publisher Services